UNITED NATIONS CONFERENCE ON TRADE AND DEVELOPMENT

UNCTAD

Twenty Years of India's Liberalization
Experiences and Lessons

Edited By
Rashmi Banga and Abhijit Das

uOttawa
LIBRARIES

Centre for
WTO
Studies

विश्व व्यापार संगठन अध्ययन केन्द्र

DÉPÔT
DEPOSIT

UNITED NATIONS
New York and Geneva, 2012

Symbols of United Nations documents are composed of capital letters combined with figures. Mention of such a symbol indicates a reference to a United Nations document.

The views expressed in this book are those of the authors and do not necessarily reflect the views of the UNCTAD secretariat. The designations employed and the presentation of the material in this publication do not imply the expression of any opinion whatsoever on the part of the Secretariat of the United Nations concerning the legal status of any country, territory, city or area, or of its authorities, or concerning the delimitation of its frontiers or boundaries.

Material in this publication may be freely quoted; acknowledgement, however, is requested (including reference to the document number). It would be appreciated if a copy of the publication containing the quotation were sent to the Publications Assistant, Division on Globalization and Development Strategies, UNCTAD, Palais des Nations, CH-1211 Geneva

UNITED NATIONS PUBLICATION

UNCTAD/OSG/2012/1

Sales No. E.12.II.D.9

ISBN 978-92-1-112852-9

e-ISBN 978-92-1-055503-6

CONTENTS

ACKNOWLEDGEMENTS

We are extremely grateful to Richard Kozul Wright, Head, Economic Cooperation and Integration among Developing Countries, and Rajeev Kher, Additional Secretary, Department of Commerce, Government of India, for their unstinted support and guidance in this endeavour. We are also highly thankful to the contributors, who accepted this very arduous and challenging task and enriched the book with their valuable insights. The timely revisions made by the contributors are much appreciated.

The chapters in the book were presented at an international conference jointly organised by Centre for WTO Studies, New Delhi, and UNCTAD. The authors are grateful for the comments and suggestions received from Narhari Rao, Deputy Country Director, ADB; K.L. Krishna, former Professor, Delhi School of Economics; Manoj Pant, Professor, Jawaharlal Nehru University; B.N. Goldar, Professor, Institute of Economic Growth, and other participants of the conference.

We are grateful to Manisha Jain for copy-editing the book.

The Editors

ABBREVIATIONS AND ACRONYMS

CRR	Cash Reserve Ratio
ERP	Effective Rate of Protection
EXIM	Export Import Bank of India
ELG	Export-Led Growth
FI	Financial Institution
FDI	Foreign Direct Investment
FERA	Foreign Exchange Regulation Act
FII	Foreign Institutional Investors
MEP	minimum export price
ICICI	Industrial Credit and Investment Corporation of India Ltd.
NSE	National Stock Exchange of India
NBFC	Non-Banking Finance Company
OECD	Organization for Economic Co-operation and Development
OFDI	Outward FDI
QC	Quantity Ceiling
QR	Quantitative Restrictions
RBI	Reserve Bank of India
SLR	Statutory Liquidity Ratio
SEBI	The Securities and Exchange Board of India
TFP	Total Factor Productivity
UTI	Unit Trust of India

ABOUT THE AUTHORS

- *Abhijit Das* is Professor and Head, Centre for WTO Studies, Indian Institute of Foreign Trade, New Delhi. Earlier, he was Officer-in-Charge of UNCTAD's India project.

- *Arvind Virmani* is Affiliate Professor (and Distinguished Senior Fellow), George Mason University (School of Public Policy-CEMP), and Executive Director (India, Bangladesh, Bhutan and Sri Lanka), International Monetary Fund. He is former Chief Economic Advisor in Ministry of Finance, India.

- *Partha Ray* is Professor, Indian Institute of Management Calcutta, India. He is former Director, Department of Economic Policy & Research, Reserve Bank of India.

- *Ramesh Chand* is Director, National Centre for Agricultural Economics and Policy Research, New Delhi. He is former National Professor of Indian Council of Agricultural Research and has served as Professor and Head, Agricultural Economics Unit at the Institute of Economic Growth, India.

- *Rashmi Banga* is Economic Affairs Officer, Economic Cooperation and Integration of Developing Countries, UNCTAD. She is former Officer-in-Charge and Senior Economist in UNCTAD's India project and Associate Professor at Jawaharlal Nehru University.

- *Subhash C. Ray* is Professor of Economics, University of Connecticut, USA. He has been visiting faculty to Department of Econometrics, University of Sydney, Australia; Department of Statistics and Operational Research, University of Alicante, Spain; Indian Institute of Management, Ahmedabad and Calcutta, India.

- *Sumedha Bajar* is a Research Scholar at the Institute for Social and Economic Change, Bangalore.

I.
Overview

India's growth miracle has attracted worldwide attention, particularly because this growth has been pursuant to the wide ranging economic reforms introduced in the early 1990s. Many other developing countries intensified Liberalization during this period but were unable to experience a similar spurt in their economic growth. One distinctive feature of Indian Liberalization experience is the gradual and calibrated manner in which reforms were introduced, especially with respect to external Liberalization, be it in the financial, agricultural or manufacturing sector. On the risk of being categorised as "reluctant globaliser", India embarked on the path of slow and steady Liberalization and still maintains high tariffs in many agricultural products and has given limited access to foreign investors in many sectors. To what extent has this approach stimulated economic growth in India? This book is a modest attempt to capture the role played by trade and foreign direct investment (FDI) polices in growth and development of different sectors in India.

After pursuing a strategy of self-reliance for more than forty years, compelled by the balance-of- payment crisis, India initiated wide-ranging economic reforms in 1991. These reforms covered macro-economic stabilization programmes addressing fiscal and current-account imbalances and exchange rate regime. These reforms also sought to evolve an industrial and trade policy framework to promote efficiency, reduce the bias in favour of excessive capital intensity and encourage an employment-oriented industrialization. Reforms in industrial policies provided the direction for reforms in other areas such as trade and finance. Industrial reforms sought primarily to remove licensing requirements, which posed significant barriers to entry, and prevented the manufacturing sector from taking advantage of economies of scale. Industrial de-licensing, which was initiated in 1984-85, was initially confined to a few sectors. The new industrial policy of 24 July 1991 significantly expanded the coverage of industrial sectors that were de-licensed. It also sought substantially to deregulate industry to promote the growth of a more efficient and competitive industrial economy.

Simultaneously, trade policy Liberalization sought to create an environment to provide a stimulus to export and reduce the degree of regulation and licensing control on foreign trade. This was achieved by progressively dismantling the complex system of import licensing, phased reduction in customs duty and the gradual removal of quantitative restrictions on imports. The past two decades of trade Liberalization have also coincided with India taking binding obligations at the multilateral and bilateral levels. Multilaterally, as a result of the Uruguay Round of Multilateral Trade Negotiations, India bound its customs duty on two thirds of the industrial products. Also, being a participant to the WTO's Information Technology Agreement, India eliminated tariffs on abroad range of information technology (IT) products. At the bilateral level, India gradually allowed zero duty imports on substantially all trade from Sri Lanka, Singapore, SAFTA, ASEAN, Korea, Japan and Malaysia.

Steps were also taken to facilitate the inflow of FDI. These included raising the limit of foreign equity holdings from 40 to 51 per cent in a wide range of priority industries; streamlining procedures for investment in non-priority industries, and establishing the Foreign Investment Promotion Board to expedite the clearances required. India has progressively increased autonomous Liberalization in many services sub-sectors under Mode 3 of trade in services. Reforms in the financial sector included phasing in of prudential norms for income recognition, classification of assets and provisioning for bad debts, revised formats for making the balance sheet and profit and loss accounts to reflect the actual financial health and a time schedule for attaining 8 per cent capital to risk-weighted assets for scheduled commercial banks. The statutory liquidity ratio (SLR) and cash reserve ratio (CRR), which once amounted to 63 per cent combined pre-emption of incremental deposits, were brought down to reduce the pre-emption of bank credit by Government and government borrowing was undertaken at market interest rates. To increase competition in the banking system, the Reserve Bank of India (RBI) granted licenses to several private banking operations. The aggregate foreign investment in a private bank from all sources could be up to 74 per cent of the paid-up capital. At least 26 per cent of the paid-up capital was to be held by residents, except in case of a wholly owned subsidiary of a foreign bank.

India undertook far reaching reforms in other sectors as well. For instance, in the telecommunications sector, which was state-owned until 1991, private participation was gradually introduced by inviting bids for non-exclusive licenses to provide cellular services in Delhi, Mumbai, Kolkata and Chennai. Over the past two decades the market has graduated from being one where competition was limited by design to one where entry restrictions have been phased out to embrace the competitive model.

Following the reforms of 1990s, the Indian economy has enjoyed a strong growth with the average annual growth exceeding 8 per cent since 2003. Even amidst the global slowdown, its real GDP grew by 8.8 per cent in 2010. In 2011, India's growth is likely to have slowed to 7.6 per cent.[1] Nevertheless, overall this has been a very impressive performance, which has translated into a strong rise in average real per capita income. The real per capita income grew from 3.2 per cent in the 1980s to 3.6 per cent in 1990s and surged to 5.4 per cent in the 2000s. This has been accompanied by a decline in poverty ratio from 45 per cent in 1993-94 to 32 per cent in 2009-10[2] and a double digit growth in 2004-09 for some poor states of India, including Bihar and Orissa. Investment as a percentage of GDP has also grown from 27 per cent in 2002-03 to 35 per cent in 2010-11. Private investments have grown very fast and have always been higher than public sector investments since 1987-88. Private investments constituted around 80 per cent of total investments in 2010-11. Domestic savings in the 2000s represented a substantial 31 per cent of the GDP and provided a significant part of the investment. Increasing per capita income with a corresponding rise in per capita consumption and private investment has generated a strong domestic demand, the driving force of behind India's growth.

This growth process has been accompanied by some unique structural changes. Particularly, the share of services in the total GDP increased from 43 per cent in 1990-91 to 58 per cent in 2010-11, whereas agriculture's share declined from 28 per cent to 14 per cent and the manufacturing sector's share remained more or less the same (28 per cent). Unlike the experience of other developing countries, the industrial sector does not appear to be the core of India's growth dynamics. Although the industrial sector's contribution to total output remained more or less the same, this does not imply that the sector did not contribute to the growth process. In fact, it grew fast but not as fast as the services sector. From 2000-01 to 2010-11, agriculture grew on an average 2.2 per cent annually, industrial sector at a rate of 7.7 per cent and services sector, 8.7 per cent, contributing more than 80 per cent of GDP growth.[3] This led many to term India's growth as "services-led growth".

Some other features of the services-led growth in India are worth noting: a) The growth of services has been the least volatile as compared with the other sectors; b) The sector has a declining capital-output ratio and

c) the services sector's growth has a high correlation with other sectors' growth[4]. Another important feature of India's growth is the lack of change in the sectoral employment pattern over time. The increase in the contribution of services to total output has not been accompanied by an equally impressive increase in its contribution to total employment. Its declining capital-output ratio has not translated to any significant rise in its employment intensity. Agriculture still contributes around 50 per cent of total employment, terming India's growth as "jobless growth".

In India's external sector, the ratio of trade in goods and services to GDP increased from an average of 15 per cent in the 1980s to 39per cent in the decade of 2000, indicating closer commercial links between India and the global economy since 1991. The trends in India's international trade over the past three decades provide useful messages. First, despite significant policy changes during 1990s aimed at dismantling import barriers, the annual average growth in imports was 8 per cent, which was 1 percentage point lower than the import growth in the 1980s. Import compression during the 1990s appears to have adversely affected the export performance, as the average annual export growth during this decade was only marginally higher than that of the previous decade. Second, the removal of quantitative restrictions, lowering of customs duties and simplification of tax administration during the 2000s appear to have been more instrumental in boosting imports, compared with Liberalization measures taken during the 1990s. The average annual growth of import touched 21 per cent in this decade. This eased the import compression witnessed during the previous decade and facilitated the exporters to obtain inputs and intermediates at competitive prices from global sources. The annual export growth surged to 19 per cent during the 2000s. This suggests that India's export performance may have been crucially dependent on, and triggered by, the availability of imported inputs at competitive prices.

Third, in contrast to the 1980s, services exports grew faster than goods exports during the 1990s and 2000s. Harnessing advancements in information technology and communication over the past decade, India has become a significant exporter of IT and IT-Enabled Services (ITES). It has been estimated that India has a lion's share of 35 per cent in the global BPO market[5] and 24 per cent share in computer and information services[6]. While India has managed to successfully ride on the BPO boom and has emerged as a dynamic economy in this segment, on the flip side, this has resulted in increased reliance on IT and ITES services in total services export. With almost 45 per cent of services exports accounted for by IT and ITES exports, coupled with their concentration in a few markets, the overall performance of India's services exports crucially depends on developments in domestic regulations and restrictions on BPO in a few developed countries.

Fourth, in the near future, India's overall export performance would be increasingly determined by the overall performance of its services exports. While the value of goods exports has been significantly higher than that of services exports over the past three decades, the weight of services exports in total exports has shot up from around 20 per cent in the 1990s to around 32 per cent in the 2000s. Keeping global services markets open and preventing new restrictions on services imports in developed countries becomes a key imperative of India's commercial diplomacy. Also, with companies in South East Asia becoming global BPO players, Indian BPO companies would need to quickly climb the ladder and provide more value-added services. Simultaneously, they also need to explore services which are still in the pioneer stage, have limited suppliers in a few locations and thus provide vast untapped potential for future growth.

Another significant change in the economy over the past two decades has been with respect to FDI, both inward as well as outbound. Prior to the initiation of economic reforms, annual FDI was less than $100 million. However, since 1991, FDI flows have surged over 100-fold and are now around $35 billion. Notwithstanding a minor reversal in this trend during 2010–11, the trend over the past 20 years indicates foreign investors' increased confidence in India's economic prospects. India is gradually emerging as a source of global capital as a large number of Indian firms in multitude sectors are investing abroad in both developed and developing countries. On an annual basis, outward FDI (OFDI) was less than $0.5 billion at the beginning of the reform period but progressively increased to around $20 billion during 2008–09. Another noticeable trend is that the direction of OFDI has changed over the years. Till 2003, around 70 per cent of India's total OFDI went to developed countries. However, by 2007, almost 60 per cent of the OFDI was directed towards Africa, Eastern Europe and the Commonwealth of Independent States and Latin America.

It would not be incorrect to state that India's growth strategy and trajectory differs significantly from the path followed by other Asian countries, particularly South East Asian and Far Eastern economies, in at least three key respects. First, India's growth has been led by domestic demand and not by exports. This has partially insulated the economy from global upheavals and downturns. Second, unlike other Asian economies that have relied on the manufacturing sector, the growth of Indian economy has been increasingly propelled by the booming services sector. Third, unlike most of the East Asian economies which have integrated with global production networks, India has largely remained outside such production-sharing arrangements.

While it would be an extremely challenging analytical exercise to attribute the extent of changes in the economy to specific initiatives under the Liberalization process, it cannot be denied that Liberalization has contributed substantially to the high growth trajectory of the Indian economy. Further, the pace, sequence and extent of Liberalization helped. Against this backdrop, this book anchors its analysis in calibrated financial and trade Liberalization policies and explores their impact on the growth of the manufacturing, agriculture and financial sectors. Specifically, some of the issues probed are the role played by trade Liberalization in the growth of the manufacturing sector, agricultural Liberalization in balancing consumer and producer interests and FDI in improving the productivity of the banking sector. Based on India's experiences, it also seeks to derive some of the important lessons learnt in the process, which can benefit other developing countries. The chapter scheme is as follows:

Chapter II by Rashmi Banga and Abhijit Das, assess the impact of trade policies since 1991 on the manufacturing sector's growth. It traces trade-related reforms since 1991 and highlights some specific export promotion policies. One of the key issues examined is the role played by growth in exports, imports and domestic demand in the overall growth of the manufacturing sector. To identify the impact of trade policies on shifts in the manufacturing sector's growth trajectory, the year of structural breaks in the growth of overall manufacturing sector and that of the organised manufacturing sector, are identified for the period 1950-51 to 2008-09. This chapter also undertakes a similar analysis for identifying the years of structural breaks in the growth of real exports and real imports. Assuming that significant changes in policies related to international trade would have commensurate impacts on trade flows, the chapter examines the association, if any, between the years of structural breaks in manufacturing growth and trade growth. It also uses co-integration analysis for identifying the long-term and short-term relationships and causality between export and import growth with manufacturing growth. Finally, it identifies success stories in the manufacturing sector, where trade boosted growth. The chapter concludes by drawing broad lessons learnt from India's experience of trade Liberalization.Tracing the slow and gradual dismantling of trade barriers and using sophisticated econometric tools to identify structural breaks and causality in growth of trade and output, the authors conclude that the growth of the Indian manufacturing sector has not been led by exports but by imports and domestic demand. Gradual tariff Liberalization in key sectors induced the required competition in the domestic market and improved the overall growth performance.

Prior to the economic Liberalization of 1991, the main objective of India's agricultural trade policy was apparently to manage fluctuations in domestic supply. This was achieved by controlling imports on the basis of quantitative restrictions, which largely insulated the domestic market from international agriculture markets. However, with the removal of quantitative restrictions on 1729 products, there was likely to be greater integration between domestic and international prices. In this context, Chapter III by Ramesh Chand and Sumedha Bajar, highlight how trade policies in the agriculture sector have been used to protect consumers from abnormal increases in global prices. The chapter highlight the fact that the objective of India's trade policy has gradually changed and expanded in scope over the past twenty years. The central theme of this chapter is to discern how India has balanced the interest of producers and consumers with the progressive Liberalization of trade since 1991. The authors highlight the twin challenges in this respect: the need for maintaining a stable and remunerative price environment for the benefit of producers and preventing any significant increase in prices, which the vulnerable consumer is not in a position to absorb. They assert that the guiding principle for agricultural trade Liberalization has been to allow domestic prices to move in tandem with the trend in global prices but to insulate it against sharp spike and troughs. This seeks to prevent a steep hike in domestic prices due to transmission of global price effect. Nevertheless, the authors note that import Liberalization that results in the lower-

ing of domestic prices is favourable to consumers but adversely affects producers. In this context, the authors also discuss the debate surrounding the use of trade policy instruments, particularly customs tariff, as an alternative to buffer stocks for domestic price stabilization, particularly for rice and wheat. This is particularly relevant against the backdrop of frequent and severe supply and price shocks at the domestic and global level. Finally, the authors draw some important lessons learnt from India's strategic approach towards agriculture trade Liberalization.

Chapter IV by Partha Ray and Arvind Virmani, discusses the achievements and pitfalls of India's financial sector policies and the situation during the 1970s and 1980s. This provides the relevant context for examining the impact of various policy initiatives aimed at financial sector Liberalization taken since 1991 covering banks, development financial institutions, mutual funds, non-bank financial companies, insurance, financial markets and capital account Liberalization. The authors examine the impact of various diverse elements of financial sector Liberalization in India. They assess the impact of banking reforms by considering outcome indicators, such as interest rate deregulation, reduction in statutory pre-emption, prudential measures and health of Indian banking and ownership structure of Indian banking. While comprehensively analysing the four constituents of Indian financial markets -money market, bond market, foreign exchange market and stock market – the authors highlight that financial markets have undergone reforms of far reaching significance. Overall, the authors are of the view that financial Liberalization in India improved the allocation of funds and allowed the economy to reap the benefits of static welfare efficiency; but reforms that could increase competitive supply of funds to new entrepreneurs, credit rationed producers and (direct) investors have been somewhat limited. They conclude that the calibrated pace of reform ensured the safety and stability of the financial system and did not involve policy reversals.

Chapter V by Subhash C. Ray, assesses the role of India's Liberalization policies for the banking sector in the banking sector's performance. Tracing the various banking sector reforms over the years, it highlights that unlike many developing countries, the banking sector reforms in India were a deliberate and gradualist attempt to allow greater role for private and foreign banks so as to improve efficiency through competition. Using a non- parametric approach and carefully selected indicators of performance, the author compares total factor productivity growth and technical efficiency in public sector banks, private banks and foreign banks in the post-reform period. The author also discusses whether the foreign ownership of equity matters; whether foreign banks provide better quality of service; and the role played by schemes such as voluntary retirement scheme in infusing productivity growth in public sector banks. The author highlights the lessons learnt from the Liberalization process of the banking sector of India.

The important message which comes out from the chapter is that though foreign equity matters and helps in improving the performance indices, FDI in banking may not be vital for improving the performance of the banking sector as a whole. Public sector banks may perform better than foreign banks and also domestic private sector banks if competition is gradually infused in the market. The results of the non-parametric analysis show that there has been a general increase in total factor productivity of all categories of banks in the post-reform period. The rate of productivity growth was higher among foreign banks than among domestic banks. Improvement in technical efficiency was a main factor behind productivity growth. However, as a group, public sector banks were more efficient than foreign banks. This superior performance of public sector banks was evident despite State Bank of India, the iconic bank in that category, being excluded from the analysis. Private domestic banks were substantially less efficient than foreign banks. In a direct comparison of the three leading banks from the different ownership groups, ICICI Bank from the private domestic category had the highest total factor productivity. HSBC, a major foreign bank, came a close second, while SBI was a distant third. The one-time voluntary retirement scheme launched in 2000 to downsize employment seems to have paid off in the form of improved total factor productivity down the road. A higher share of foreign ownership of equity has had a beneficial impact on the efficiency of a bank. This is true for both private and public sector banks. When adjusted for quality (based on the average number of customer complaints registered with the Banking Ombudsman Office), the efficiency of foreign banks is much lower than what was otherwise found for 2009. This is in conflict with the popular perception that foreign banks offer a higher quality of customer service.

Overall, all of the chapters emphasise the gradual and calibrated approach taken by India's policymakers with respect to Liberalization in different sectors. Financial Liberalization has also followed a similar path. All of the chapters arrive at strikingly similar conclusions, which point towards the benefits of this approach to the economy. Using different tools of analysis, the authors conclude that the growth of the sector concerned was not hindered by the reforms undertaken in terms of Liberalization with respect to trade and FDI. In fact, the gradual calibrated and sequential Liberalization, compared with across-the-board quick and extensive Liberalization followed by many developing countries, played a vital role in the growth process of the Indian economy. This is an important learning from India's experience and may be useful to other developing countries that still enjoy a window of policy space with respect to certain sectors in the economy.

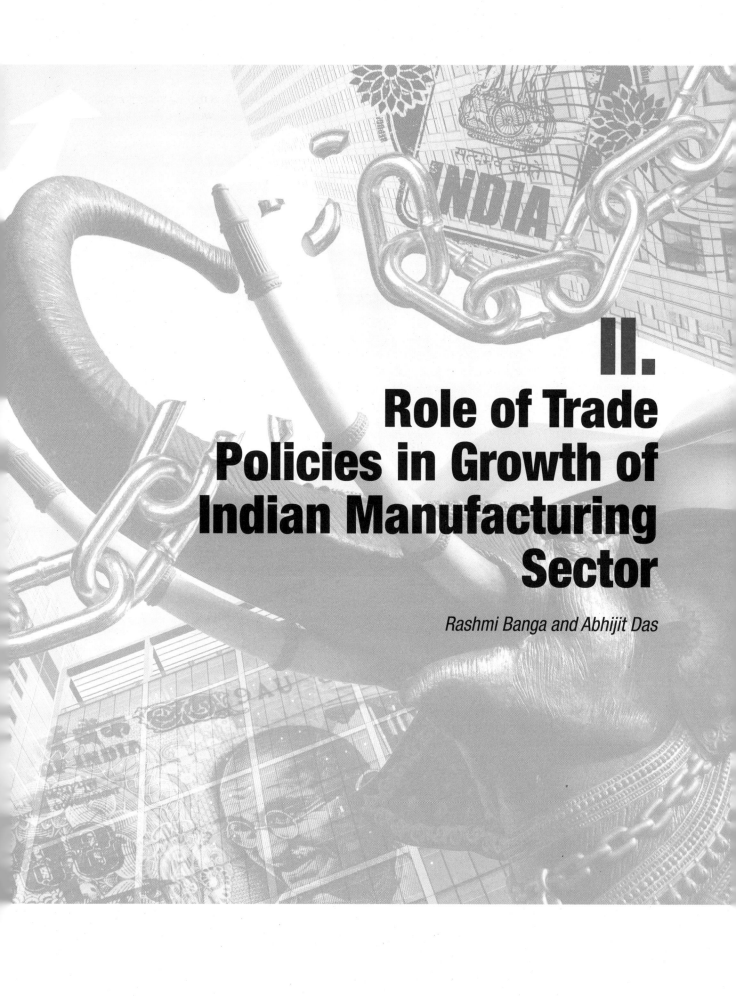

II.
Role of Trade
Policies in Growth of
Indian Manufacturing
Sector

Rashmi Banga and Abhijit Das

A. Introduction

Manufacturing sector in India, compared with the other sectors, has always been the main focus of Liberalization policies. From import substitution policies of the 1950s to export promotion strategies of the 1980s and to major tariff Liberalization of the 1990s, the sector has experienced a wide variety of policy interventions. However, this sector has also been of major concern owing to its sticky growth rates, decade after decade, and persistently low contribution to total output and employment in the economy. The sector's average annual growth rate remained around 5.8 per cent in the 1950s and 1960s, falling to 5 per cent in the 1970s and returning to 5.8 per cent in the 1980s.[7] The sector's contribution to GDP varied from 12 per cent to 14 per cent from the 1960s till the 1980s and its contribution to total employment remained low with negative growth in the 1980s (-0.12 per cent per annum).

The reforms of 1990s were accompanied by an improvement in the value added growth rate of the manufacturing sector as it touched 6 per cent. Employment growth increased to 2.9 per cent per annum.[8] This led to a whole stream of literature which estimated and assessed the impact of Liberalization on the growth of output and productivity of the sector. But in spite of the reforms, it is argued that protection to the sector remained high. Many products, especially intermediate products and consumer durables, continued to enjoy high tariffs. Further, protection to the sector was provided in many other forms as well, which included non-tariff barriers, quantitative restrictions (QRs), licensing regime and selective protection which resulted in high magnitude and high variance in protection rates.

In early 2000, however, a careful dismantling of protection started. This was initiated by tariff reduction. The weighted average of tariffs declined steadily from 24 per cent in 2001 to 7 per cent in 2009. It was also brought down for consumer goods from 32 per cent in 1999 to 9.5 per cent in 2009. More important, however, quantitative restrictions were removed for all items in 2001. During the 2000s, through many complementary policies, protection to the manufacturing sector was lowered. Along with this, important steps were taken to boost manufacturing sector exports. These included discontinuing actual user conditions on Open General Licence imports and items were shifted from Restricted to Limited Permissible lists and further from Limited Permissible to Open General License scheme.

For the manufacturing sector, the obligation of importing Open General License items via EXIM scrip was also abolished in a phased manner.

Correspondingly, the manufacturing sector witnessed the most important breakthrough in its growth rate in the 2000s. The decadal average annual growth rate of the sector touched 8 per cent. The sector also witnessed a spurt in imports and exports. The average annual growth rate of manufacturing real exports[9] surged from 5 per cent in the 1980s to 9.7 per cent in the 1990s and increased further to 12 per cent in the 2000s. The average annual growth rate of real imports increased from 5.4 per cent in the 1980s to 11 per cent in the 1990s but then surged to around 16 per cent in the 2000s. Although the sector's contribution to total GDP did not increase much (mainly because of a much higher growth of services sector), its contribution to total employment witnessed a rise post 2005.

The manufacturing sector's impressive performance in the post-Liberalization period accompanied by important changes in trade policies may indicate that much of the manufacturing sector's growth can be attributed to Liberalization polices. However, the post-Liberalization period, especially the 2000s, was also a period of an unprecedented growth of the Indian economy as a whole. This growth was mainly spearheaded by the services sector growth. GDP grew at an average annual rate of 7 per cent in the 2000s compared with 5 per cent in the 1990s. More important, there was a rise in average annual growth of per capita income. These two factors contributed significantly to domestic demand expansion. Given this scenario, the extent to which Liberalization policies may have contributed to the manufacturing sector growth becomes an extremely important question to address. It is an important issue not only for India in terms of future policy directions but also for other developing countries which have limited policy tools to address their growth concerns and are looking at India's Liberalization and growth experience for some important lessons.

In this context, we attempt to find answers to the following questions:

1. Did Liberalization policies lead to a structural break in the manufacturing sector growth?
2. Has India's manufacturing growth been an export-led growth or an import-induced growth? What has been the role of domestic demand?
3. What are the successful and not so successful stories with respect to trade

policies and growth within the manufacturing sector?

4. What could be the broad lessons from India's experience of Liberalization with respect to the manufacturing sector?

To answer these questions, we use different methodologies. The impact of trade policies on the manufacturing sector is assessed by identifying the years of structural break in manufacturing sector growth from 1950–51 to 2008–09. The identification of years of structural break has been fairly commonly used in the literature to identify which set of Liberalization polices coincide with the shift in the sector's growth trajectory. We also identify the years of structural break in the growth of real exports and real imports. This is done to further narrow down the subsets of polices within the broad set of Liberalization policies that may have been more effective in leading to structural breaks in the growth of exports and imports. Two kinds of structural breaks in manufacturing sector growth have been identified to examine whether Liberalization policies were effective. These are a *gradual shift* in the mean of the series (innovational outliers) and a *sudden change* in the mean of the series (additive outliers) using Clemente *et al.*'s (1998) tests. The question whether manufacturing sector growth has been an export-led growth or an import-induced growth is addressed by estimating short-term and long-term relationships between manufacturing growth, export growth and import growth. Causality tests are undertaken to reveal the cause-and-effect relationships between manufacturing sector growth and the growth of exports and imports. A multivariate co-integration analysis is carried out by estimating Vector Error Correction Model (VECM), and Granger non-causality tests based on VAR are undertaken for testing causality in the relationships. An industry-level analysis is undertaken based on trade and production data for the organised manufacturing sector to identify industries which may have or may not have benefitted from Liberalization policies. Broad conclusions are drawn from the arrived results.

B. Cautious Liberalization and Change in the Composition of Trade

1. Reforms of 1991: Cautious and Selective

Liberalization polices in India have been generally in tandem with the industrial policies followed over years.

This may not be the case in many other developing countries. The Industrial Policy of 1948 emphasised heavy protection to the Indian industry as it aimed to build a strong heavy capital goods industrial base in the economy. However, faced with low growth rate and lack of the sector's capability to build a strong industrial base, the Industrial Policy of 1956 encouraged foreign capital. It was envisaged that foreign capital would bring better technology and lead to spill-over effects on the domestic industry. However, the still sticky growth of the sector for the next two decades led to a change in the attitudes and direction of the industrial policy, and the Industrial Policy of 1980 encouraged export-oriented industries and import of technology and raw materials.

In 1991, imports were regulated by a narrow positive list of freely importable items. Items not in the positive list were either prohibited for imports or could be imported subject to compliance with the requirements of a complex licensing system. The overall approach to import management was selective and geared to the curtailment of non-essential and low-priority imports, with particular emphasis on discouraging inventory build-up of imported inputs through the use of fiscal and monetary modes of regulation. Although multilateral trade rules of GATT in general prohibited QRs on the import or export of any product, these rules provided exceptions to this fundamental principle on balance-of-payment grounds. India resorted to the BOP exception and maintained QRs on imports on almost 80 per cent products prior to the economic reforms of 1991. This edifice of regulated trade was gradually dismantled through tariff reforms and simplification of import procedures and requirements.

The reforms of 1991 brought some major changes in the existing tariff structure. Average and weighted tariffs declined from 81.9 and 49.5 per cent in 1990 to 57.4 and 27.8 per cent in 1991, respectively (Table 1). The peak duty rate was lowered gradually from >200 per cent in 1990 to 35 per cent in 1999. A number of other changes were made to simplify the system, and many exemptions related to end use were removed. One of the most important steps undertaken in 1992 was to shift the basis of regulating imports from a positive list of freely importable items to a limited negative list in 1992. Now, except the products listed in the negative list, all other products could be freely imported.

The EXIM policy of 1992 substantially eliminated licensing and discretionary controls on trade and provided further impetus to exports. Apart from consumer goods, almost all capital goods, raw materials and intermediate goods could be freely imported subject only to payment of customs duty. For consumer goods, a major step taken was to allow their import under Special Import Licence (SIL) issued to certain categories of exporters, including deemed exporters, trading/export houses and manufacturers who had acquired ISO 9000 or BIS 14000 certification of quality. The special import licensees were freely transferable. During 1995–96, the definition of consumer goods was changed to suit importers' needs, so that they could freely import parts, components and spares of consumer goods as well. These items were earlier restricted to the extent that they could be imported without a licence only by actual users. Further, the list of freely importable consumer goods was expanded to include 78 items, which included natural essential oils, instant coffee, refrigerated trucks, cranes and other utility vehicles. By 1995, more than 3000 tariff lines covering raw materials, intermediates and capital goods were freed of import licensing requirements, and supplementary licenses for all importers except small-scale industries were abolished. In 1996, 300 items could be imported under the Special Import License. Further, studies estimating the ERP and import coverage ratios show that compared with the 1980s, ERP declined in the 1990s. It declined from 125.9 per cent in 1986–90 to 80.2 per cent in 1990–95 and further to 40.4 per cent in 1996–2000, while import coverage ratio declined from 96.1 per cent in 1986–90 to 37.9 per cent in 1990–95 and further to 24.8 per cent in 1996–2000 (Das, 2003).

2. Dismantling of Protection in 2000s

Although the reforms of 1991 brought in some important changes in the tariff regime and simplified many administrative and import controls, these reforms were not uniform across the board and continued to provide selective protection. Import restrictions on capital goods, raw materials and components were liberalised on a fast track, while import restrictions were maintained for most consumer goods. India continued to maintain quantitative restrictions on a large number of consumer goods. Consequently, the consumer goods sector was somewhat insulated from competition. In 1996, when the tariff line-wise import policy was first announced, around 40 per cent of the total tariff lines were still under QRs.

Studies that estimated nominal and effective rate of protection during the 1990s (Goldar and Hasheem, 1992; Gang and Pandey, 1998; Das, 2003) find that the effective rate of protection was still high in the 1990s. For the entire period 1980–2000, the average effective protection rate remained as high as 87.4 per cent for consumer goods and 112 per cent for intermediate goods and 95 per cent for the sector as a whole (Das, 2003). Some important export incentives were announced, such as the enhancement of Import Replenishment (REP) license entitlements to 30 per cent across-the-board for all merchandise exporters, which was later raised to 40 per cent for some sectors. In March 2000, after losing the WTO dispute against the United States on QRs, the EXIM Policy announced the removal of QRs on 714 items and the residual 715 items were liberalised by 1 April 2001. Therefore, it was only after a decade of Liberalization reforms that QRs were totally removed. The reduction in average tariffs and peak tariffs in India, though substantial, also happened in a phased manner, i.e. over almost two decades. Table 1 depicts average tariffs and peak tariffs for different years in the post-Liberalization period. Till about 2004, the average tariffs remained above 20 per cent.

In terms of simple averages, the industrial tariffs fell from a very high 82 per cent in 1990 to 33 per cent in 1999 and further to 9 per cent in 2009 for all manufactured products. In terms of weighted average, the tariffs fell from around 50 per cent in 1990 to 29 per cent in 1999 and reached 7 per cent in 2009. Peak

Table 1	Average tariffs and peak tariffs for industrial products 1990-2008 (Percentage)		
Tariff Year	**Simple**	**Weighted**	**Peak tariffs (%)**
1990	81.69	49.55	Exceeded 200
1992	57.45	27.89	150
1997	30.08	19.92	85
1999	33	28.61	35
2001	31.06	24.76	30
2004	27.87	20.95	25
2005	15.38	11.97	15
2007	13.22	8.6	12.5
2008	9.1	5.91	10
2009	9.43	7.21	

Source: World Integrated Solutions and various Economic Surveys

tariffs in industrial products were cut down from over 200 per cent in 1990 to about 30 per cent in 2001. Tariff protection declined much more slowly for consumer goods than for raw materials and intermediate products. Tariffs on capital goods were brought down much faster (Fig. 1). Although nominal tariff on consumer goods was reduced in line with those on other goods, the effective rate of tariffs on consumer goods may actually have increased for much of the 1990s because the remaining import restriction/QRs kept the effective rate of tariff protection on final consumer goods high.

Cautious Liberalization was followed across industries as well. For industries which were relatively more protected and where weighted tariffs were above 40 per cent in 1990, such as food and kindred products, textile mill products and apparel and related products, weighted tariffs remained above 40 per cent till about 2000. Tariffs were brought down to 10 per cent and below across the board after 2001 (Table 2).

Figure 1	Tariff Liberalization for capital goods, consumer goods and industrial supplies

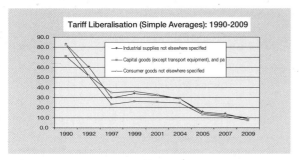

Source: World Integrated Trade Solutions

3.   Export Promotion Policies

The reforms of 1985 emphasised the export promotion of the manufacturing products. Several incentives were provided and schemes introduced to boost exports. These included Cash Compensatory Support, Replenishment import license, duty drawback, duty free licenses and income tax exemption on profits of exports. Export-processing zones provided further support to exporters for sourcing their raw materials and marketing their products. The import of capital goods and parts and accessories was made easier by exempting them from import licensing and lowering their import tariffs. The reforms of 1991 differed in nature with respect to export promotion schemes. They abolished the Cash Compensatory Support and replaced the Replenishment import license with

EXIM scrips, which allowed import of a much wider range of intermediate products. This scheme was later abolished and more incentives were provided for exports. Exporters were allowed to keep a certain percentage of their foreign exchange earned. Further, export promotion goods scheme was introduced whereby imports were linked to export obligations. An important step in export promotion was taken around the beginning of 2000s. Changes were brought in the policy of reserving production of certain items for the small-scale sector. This policy had covered about 800 items since late 1970s, where units producing these items were reserved under the category of small scale, which was defined as units where investment in plant and machinery could not exceed $250,000.

4.   Composition of Real Exports and Real Imports

Given that tariff Liberalization was selective and gradual and protection remained relatively high in the 1990s, followed by substantial tariff reduction across the board in the 2000s, it would be interesting to see how exports and imports responded to Liberalization policies. Trends in total real imports and real exports[10] of manufactured products in India show that (Fig. 2) both real exports and real imports of manufactures grew faster in the 2000s. Real exports grew at an average annual rate of 10.7 per cent in 1990s and 10.2 per cent in 2000–2009, while real imports grew at an average annual rate of 13.3 per cent. Imports of manufactures therefore increased much faster than exports of manufactures in last decade.[11]

Figure 2	Real exports and real imports of manufactures in India (Rs crore)

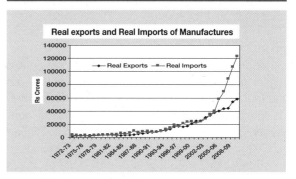

Source: Directorate General of Commercial Intelligence and Statistics (RBI- Handbook of Statistics)

Faster Liberalization of capital goods increased the import share of these products. However, the share of

Table 2	Reduction in tariffs and number of domestic peaks 1996-2008 (Percentage)							
Product Name	**Simple average**			**Weighted average**			**Number of domestic peaks**	
	1996	**2000**	**2008**	**1996**	**2000**	**2008**	**1996**	**2008**
Food and kindred products	54.2	37.7	37.7	41.2	38.9	11.7	132	2003
Tobacco manufactures	52	35.6	35.6	52	38.5	32.3	0	20
Textile mill products	50.1	9.4	9.4	45.7	27.9	9.2	0	0
Apparel and related products	50.7	10	10	51.5	37.6	10	0	0
Lumber and wood products	26.7	9.0	9.0	13.7	7.7	5.6	0	0
Furniture and fixtures	46.9	9.9	9.9	46	34.8	10	0	0
Paper and allied products	29.7	9.6	9.6	8.2	16.1	7.3	0	0
Printing, publishing, and allied	26.4	8.1	8.1	22.5	24.9	8.3	0	0
Chemicals and allied products	39.8	8.3	8.3	35.7	32.5	6.6	0	152
Petroleum refining and related	20.6	8.1	8.1	12.1	17.3	6.9	0	0

Source: World Integrated Solutions

capital goods had become almost stagnant (around 20 per cent) since 2003. Imports of intermediate goods (35 per cent) and raw materials (28 per cent) had dominated India's imports in the manufacturing sector since 1990 (Fig. 3). By 2000, together the share of raw materials and intermediate goods reached 70 per cent, while that of consumer goods and capital goods was around 15 per cent each. With the policy changes such as QR removal and grant of incentives for importing capital goods, by 2009, the share of capital goods in total imports increased to 22 per cent with the share of raw materials and intermediates of around 35 per cent each. In spite of all efforts put in since independence for import Liberalization and other reforms, the capital goods industry has not been able to achieve the levels of competitive advantages which would enable higher growth of its exports (Fig. 3). Exports from the manufacturing sector in 1988 were dominated by intermediate products (43 per cent) and consumer durables (35 per cent), and this continued till 2009, when consumer goods' share increased to 45 per cent, while that of intermediate products declined to 32 per cent. Capital goods' share increased from 6 to 13 per cent.

From this discussion, it follows that the Liberalization polices followed since the 1980s gained speed in the

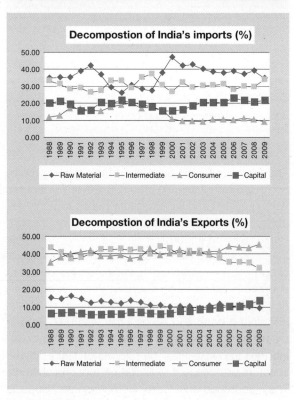

Figure 3   Imports and exports of manufacturing sector (percentage)

Source: COMTRADE, World Integrated Trade Solutions

Table 3	Sectoral contribution to total manufactures exports (Percentage)				
	1970	1980	1990	2000	2009
TOTAL	100	100	100	100	100
Coke, petroleum products and nuclear Fuel	1	0.5	3.1	3.7	14.8
Non-metallic mineral products	3.3	9.3	16.8	19	11.4
Chemicals and chemical products	3.9	5.8	9.5	10.9	11.1
Basic metals	18.6	8.3	6.2	5.8	10.4
Wearing apparel, dressing and dyeing of fur	2	9.4	15.3	15.3	7.5
Textile products	27.3	19.4	16.2	14.5	6.5
Motor vehicles, trailers and semi-trailers	2	3.5	2.3	2.4	6.3
Electrical machinery and apparatus, N.E.C	1.2	2	1.7	2.3	5.8
Machinery and equipment N.E.C.	2	3.7	3.8	3.1	4.5
Food products and beverages	19.8	18.8	9.2	7.5	3.4
Fabricated metal products	1.8	3.2	2.1	2.7	1.8
Leather and related products	6.4	6	6.1	2.9	1.3
Tobacco and related products	2.4	2.5	0.9	0.5	0.6
Others	8.3	7.6	6.7	9.4	14.6

Source: World Integrated Trade Solutions, UNCTAD

Table 4	Sectoral contribution to total manufacturing imports (Percentage)				
	1970	1980	1990	2000	2009
TOTAL	100	100	100	100	100
Coke, petroleum products and nuclear fuel	7.7	44.6	27.3	39.6	34
Machinery and equipment, N.E.C.	16.2	7.3	9.6	8.6	9.9
Chemicals and chemical products	12.8	10.8	12.3	9.3	9.9
Electrical machinery and apparatus, N.E.C	4.3	2.2	4.4	5.1	9.3
Basic metals	15.7	10.6	10.6	5.7	8.2
Non-metallic mineral products	2.1	5	9.1	11.2	6.8
Motor vehicles, trailers and semi-trailers	3	3.8	3.9	2.2	4.7
Food products and beverages	3.1	7.6	1.1	3.3	2.8
Textile products	8.3	1.8	2.1	2.6	1.3
Paper and paper products	2.3	1.6	2.1	1.5	0.9
Others	24.5	4.7	17.5	10.9	12.2
Leather and related products	6.4	6	6.1	2.9	1.3
Tobacco and related products	2.4	2.5	0.9	0.5	0.6
Others	8.3	7.6	6.7	9.4	14.6

Source: World Integrated Trade Solutions, UNCTAD

1990s and resulted in higher growth of real exports and real imports of manufactures in the 1990s than in the 1980s. However, the effective dismantling of protection started only in early 2000. This was followed by a much higher growth of imports than exports of manufactures. Further, sectoral distribution of India's exports and imports reveals some valuable information. In terms of exports, four industries comprised around 80 per cent of total exports in the 1970s: textile products, food products and beverages, basic metals and leather and leather products. Over time, the share of these industries in the export basket has declined and other industries have gained shares, such as petroleum products, chemical and chemical products, non-metallic mineral products, wearing apparels, motor vehicles and electrical machinery and apparatus. India has been able to diversify its export basket with the traditional top four exporting industries losing share from 70 per cent in the 1970s to around 20 per cent in 2009 (Table 3).

The industrial policies and trade policies of the 1960s and 1970s emphasised establishing a sound industrial base in India, accordingly in terms of imports of manufactures. In 1970 the top three industries where imports were high were machinery and equipment, basic metals and chemical and chemical products. With the changing scenario of the Indian manufacturing sector in the 1980s, the share of petroleum products rose significantly from 7 per cent in 1970 to 34 per cent in 2009. Import basket comprising manufactures has also diversified over time. In 2009, import shares are almost same for machinery and equipment and chemicals and chemical products. These rose for electrical machinery and apparatus, non-metallic mineral products, motor vehicles and also food products. This indicates that there was a rise in import competition faced by the Indian manufacturing sector with import Liberalization in the past two decades (Table 4).

C. Structural Breaks in Manufacturing Growth

Indian manufacturing sector recorded its highest-ever decadal growth rate in the 2000s. Following the global economic crisis in 2007, this sector's growth dipped but revived and clocked above 8 per cent in 2009–10 and 2010–11.[12] To trace the growth path of the Indian manufacturing sector, it is important to know that the sector has a dualistic character with a large unregistered/ unorganised sector (employing around 80 per cent of total manufacturing employment and produc-

ing around 30 per cent of total manufacturing output) coexisting with registered/organised sector. The output of the manufacturing sector therefore depends on the additive outputs of the two sub-sectors. In the past six decades, the unorganised sector's share in total value added by the manufacturing sector has declined from 59 per cent in 1950–51 to 32 per cent in 2008–09. Post 1990, the growth in organised manufacturing sector has been higher than that in the unorganised sector (Fig. 4). Most studies confine themselves to examining the organised sector's growth, mainly because of lack of time series data for the unorganised sector. We examine the growth in total manufacturing sector as well as organised manufacturing sector.

Figure 4   Growth in manufacturing real value added

Source: Central Statistical Organization, GDP by Economic Activity at 1999–2000 constant prices.

The average annual growth of real value added in total manufacturing sector increased from 5.6 per cent in the 1950s and 1960s to 6.0 per cent in the 1980s after declining to 4.2 per cent in the 1970s. The growth dipped again in the 1990s but revived to 7.4 per cent in 2000–01 to 2008–09. The average annual growth was highest in the 2000s for both organised and unorganised manufacturing sectors. It increased to 7.8 per cent for the organised manufacturing sector and 6.6 per cent for the unorganised manufacturing sector. In 2000s, both the organised and unorganised sectors experienced their highest average annual growth rates in real value added compared with the earlier decades (Table 5).

Rise in average annual growth in the real value added of the organised manufacturing sector in the 1980s and then a fall in the 1990s has been an area of much debate and discussions in India. The reforms of 1990s were expected to propel growth in the manufacturing sector but were accompanied by a fall in the decadal growth rate. Studies using different methodologies and periodization have analysed these reforms' im-

Table 5	Decadal growth in value added in manufacturing sector of India at 1999–2000 constant prices (Percentage)		
	Manufacturing sector	Organised manufacturing	Unorganised manufacturing
1950s	5.6	6.3	5.0
1960s	5.7	7.0	3.9
1970s	4.2	4.1	4.3
1980s	6.0	8.0	3.4
1990s	5.4	5.9	4.4
2000–07	7.4	7.8	6.6

Source: CSO, GDP at constant prices (1999–2000) by economic activity.
Note: Growth rates for each year are arrived at by taking natural logs and then difference from the subsequent year. For total manufacturing value added, the period is 2000–08.

pact on the sector's growth and productivity. A major area of contention in this literature is whether Liberalization reforms of the 1980s led to productivity growth in the manufacturing sector or whether 1990s reforms were more effective in raising productivity growth and hence overall growth of the sector.

Goldar and Mitra (2002) and Trivedi *et al.* (2011) provide an extensive review of this literature. According to Trivedi (2011) a consensus seems to have emerged from the literature on this issue as most studies, using different methodologies and data sources, find that total factor productivity growth (TFPG) decelerated during the 1990s compared with the 1980s. This may have been the major cause of a dip in the overall growth rate of the sector in the 1990s. Studies estimating productivity growth in the 2000s are limited. Virmani and Hashim (2011) estimate total factor productivity growth for the period 1981–82 to 1990–91, 1991–92, 1997–98 and 2002–03 to 2007–08 and find TFPG to decelerate from 0.61 per cent in the 1980s to 0.25 per cent in the 1990s but increase to 1.41 per cent in the 2000s. They term this the *"J-curve of Productivity Growth"*, where productivity growth first declines and then rises with a lag after major Liberalization reforms are undertaken since this requires a structural transformation of the economy. It is clear from this literature that Liberalization and related reforms played a very important role in the manufacturing sector's growth. However, since these reforms have been spread over two and a half decades (1985 onwards) and differ in nature, magnitude and their impact within the sector, studies using different periods of analysis have arrived

at conflicting results with respect to reforms' impact on the sector's productivity and overall growth. In this context, it becomes utmost important to identify the year of structural break in the manufacturing sector's growth. This will help identify the set of Liberalization polices that was more effective in generating growth. This may be of interest to not only Indian policymakers but also other developing countries.

Regarding the Indian economy's overall GDP growth, many studies have identified the year of structural break (e.g. Balakrishnan, 2007; Virmani, 2006; Ghatak, 1997). However, few studies have tested for the structural breaks in the manufacturing sector. Virmani (2005) tests for structural break in the growth of value added of the manufacturing sector from 1965 to 2003 and finds a potential structural break in 1981. He concludes that the removal of some of the barriers to growth imposed during 1965–80 had a greater role to play in the acceleration of manufacturing growth from 1981–82 than the simulation of new growth impulses from 1981–82. However, Wallack (2003) does not find any significant structural break in industrial growth for 1951–2001. These studies have used some variants of Chow Tests, which requires knowing the number of breakpoints and their exact location in the data series. More important, Chow test is a multivariate test and can identify structural break only with reference to a regression equation. To identify structural breaks, we use tests developed by Clement *et al.* (1998), which identify multiple structural breaks in the series. Two kinds of structural breaks are identified: *sudden shift*, or instantaneous shock that shifts the mean of the series through AO (additive outliers)[13] model, and *gradual shift*, i.e. when the shock persists and dynamically adds to change the mean of the series over the rest of the period through IO (innovational outliers) model. One important advantage of these models are that they can identify more than one structural break in the series and also identify the years of the break. Structural breaks with respect to gradual shifts (IO model) are considered more apt for tracking the policy impacts than AO models as these breaks show that whatever change happened during that year adds to the future growth of the series.

We apply these tests to identify structural breakpoints in the growth of real value added in total manufacturing sector and organised manufacturing sector. The period of analysis is 1950–51 to 2008–09 for total manufacturing sector. One of the limitations of data on value added in total manufacturing sector is that they use single deflation method in arriving at the value added. Using a double deflation method, we arrive at value added of the organised manufacturing sector. The data for the organised sector are drawn from Annual Survey of Industries from 1981–82 to 2008–09. The results of the AO[14] and IO[15] models for total manufacturing sector show that the sudden breaks in growth of value addition came in 1977 and 1997, while the structural break in the growth of real value added of manufacturing sector that added dynamically to the rest of the series and led to a gradual shift of the mean of the series came in 1991 (Table 6 and Fig. 5). The year 1974 is also identified as a break point but is not found to be statistically significant. The two results together provide an important insight. The reforms of 1980s do not appear to have led to any sudden shift or gradual shift in value added growth of total manufacturing sector. However, the 1991 reforms appear to have played a very important role in initiating a shift in the average growth of value added of the manufacturing sector. The double deflated value added series arrived for the organised manufacturing sector using data for the period 1981–82 to 2008–09 from Annual Survey of Industries[16] (which is used by most of the studies estimating productivity growth) show that there were two structural breaks in the value added growth of organised manufacturing sector. Sudden breaks in real value added growth of the organised manufacturing sector are found in 1991 and 1998, while gradual shifts in the mean of the series came around 1986 and 2001. These results support the results arrived by the studies that find the 1980s reforms as having played an important role in productivity growth of the organised manufacturing sector.

One of the important policy interventions which may have contributed to the gradual shift in the growth series of organised manufacturing sector is industrial de-licensing initiated in 1980s, which gathered momentum in 1990s. The manufacturing sector in India was significantly shackled by the licensing system that specified the limit of output of each plant. Based on the specified output, every plant was allocated a fixed quantity of crucial inputs such as cement, steel, coal, fuel, and furnace oil. Industrial de-licensing, initiated in 1984–85, removed constraints on output, inputs, location and technology, allowing the manufacturing sector to take advantage of economies of scale. Free entry into de-licensed industries also enhanced domestic competition. Cumulatively, about 23 per cent of output had been de-licensed by 1990. The process of de-licensing gathered momentum in 1991, when substantially the entire manufacturing sector, with the

exception of 16 per cent of output, was de-licensed. Some of the remaining industries were de-licensed in 1993–94.[17] Although the structural breaks in the series provide some useful insights to the growth paths and one can relate the identified breaks with the policies adopted during that period, caution needs to be taken with respect to the conclusions drawn. Structural breaks may occur due to combinations of various factors which may be internal as well as external to the economy. While important policy changes may occur during the period identified as structural break period, it cannot be conclusively said that the structural break occurred due to the change in the policy regime. However, it is plausible that the change which occurs and is sustained is because of the change in the policy regime.

Accordingly, the industrial policy of 1980s, which encouraged export-oriented production and import of technology, appears to have had a greater impact on the organised sector than on the unorganised sector. The reforms of 1980s therefore did not appear to have led to major changes in total manufacturing growth. This is also validated by the decadal growth rates of organised and unorganised sectors. The decadal growth in the 1980s increased for the organised sector but declined for the unorganised sector. This is probably the reason for lack of any structural break for total manufacturing sector in the 1980s. However, the reforms of 1990s, which were relatively broader in scope than the reforms of 1980s, appear to have encouraged growth of organised as well as unorganised sector leading to a structural break with a gradual shift in the mean of the growth of the value added series for total manufacturing sector.

The structural break that led to a gradual shift in value added growth of organised manufacturing sector in the year 2001 is an important result, as in the 2000s growth in organised manufacturing sector was much higher than the unorganised sector and its contribution to GDP also rose steadily. Decadal average annual growth rate in value added in total manufacturing has also been highest for 2000s. In the earlier section, the reforms of 1990s and 2000s were discussed. It was concluded that the reforms of 1990s were much more drastic and broader in scope than the reforms of 1980s but they were also cautious and selective in nature. Although a number of changes were introduced in the tariff structure, the effective rate of protection remained relatively high in this decade and high tariff protection continued for consumer goods. In the 2000s, the dismantling of protection was much more

Table 6	Break points using AO and IO models in real manufacturing value added				

Value added in	Breakpoints by AO model	T-Stat (P-value)	Breakpoints by IO model	T-Stat (P-value)
Value added total manufacturing sector	1977	10.99(0.00)	1974	1.28(0.20)
	1997	6.52(0.00)	1991	2.80(0.007)
Value added in organised manufacturing sector using double deflation method (based on ASI)	1991	6.29(0.00)	1986	1.98(0.06)
	1998	4.74(0.00)	2001	2.21(0.03)

effective as many non-tariff barriers were lowered and quantitative restrictions were removed. Structural break that persists in its effect on total manufacturing sector's growth rate occurred in 1991, while that in organised sector's growth, it occurred in 1986 and 2001.

To come to any plausible linkages between the structural breaks and effectiveness of trade policies in the manufacturing sector's growth, it is important to also assess the effectiveness of these policies with respect to increasing exports and imports. We undertake similar analysis with respect to real exports and real imports of manufactures to identify the years of structural breaks in these series. It would be interesting to see if the years of structural breaks in exports and imports growths coincide with the policy changes with respect to tariff Liberalization and export promotion.

The results of AO and IO models show that with respect to the growth of real exports instantaneous breaks came in 1996 and 2001 (Table 7), while the gradual additive shifts in export growth occurred in 2001. The industrial policy of export promotion of the 1980s does not seem to have played an important role in terms of causing a structural break in export growth but policies followed from 2000 onwards appear to have played a role. Although export promotion has been an objective of trade policy for a long time and incentives have been introduced for export promotion, it is difficult to say that the policy regime changed drastically in the 2000s. The role of external demand may have been more important in this decade leading to structural break in the export growth of manufactures. Some of the important policies which may have contributed were removal of items such as garments, shoes, toys and auto components from the small-scale reserved list in 2001.

Regarding imports of manufactures, sudden shifts appear in 1974 and 2002, while gradual shifts appear post 1975 and 2003 (Table 7). The additive structural break which led to the gradual shift in real imports came in 2003. Tariff Liberalization gathered speed after 2001 when across the board tariffs in the manufactures; especially consumer durables were brought down to 10 per cent. This period also coincides with the policy of removal of quantitative restrictions (2001 and 2002) on consumer durables and a spurt in imports of capital goods and machinery.

Figure 5	Structural breaks in value added of total manufacturing sector: IO model

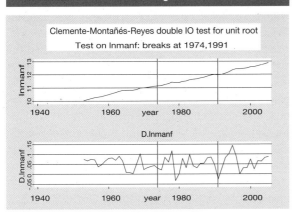

Figure 6	Structural breaks in value added of organised manufacturing sector: IO model

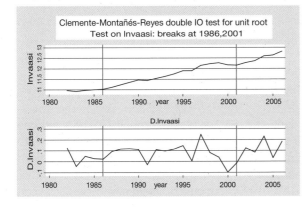

Table 7	Structural breaks in real exports and real imports			
	Breakpoints by AO model	T-Stat (P-value)	Breakpoints by IO model	T-Stat (P-value)
Real exports	1996	2.96(0.01)	1974	1.59(0.12)
	2001	4.96(0.00)	2001	3.25(0.00)
Real imports	1974	1.82(0.07)	1975	2.05(0.04)
	2002	8.12(0.00)	2003	4.65(0.00)

These results indicate that the value added growth in total manufacturing sector underwent a structural break in 1991, which changed the growth trajectory of the sector; the value added growth in the organised sector experienced a similar structural break in 2001. The year 2001 was also an important break point for the growth of real exports, while 2003 was an important break point in the growth of real imports. Together these results indicate that though the policies with respect to Liberalization started with the Industrial Policy of 1980, it was only after two decades, i.e. around the beginning of 2000, that more effective trade policies were followed which, produced the desired results in exports and imports. Import competition as well as export growth increased post 2001, which may have ignited higher value added growth in the organised manufacturing sector.

D. Is Manufacturing Growth an Export-Led Growth or an Import-Induced Growth?

Both exports and imports play an important role in the growth of any sector. However, the relative importance of the two for economy's growth is an important issue, especially at times of increased volatility in the world economy. Further, knowledge of the direction of causality of the relationship between export/import growth and growth of the sector is necessary for future policy directions. Export-led growth (ELG) literature is extensive and is based primarily on the Keynes theory, where in a particular economy demand drives the economic system to which supply adjusts, as opposed to Say's law, wherein supply creates its own demand. It is argued that developing countries lack demand, which is required for growth in the long run. If these countries produce below their productive capacities (given the surplus labour), the growth of the economy will be determined by the growth of external demand (Thirlwal, 1994). To bring about a structural change in the growth trajectory of the developing countries, one

of the driving forces suggested is therefore increase in external demand or exports.

The proponents of trade as an engine of growth found empirical support in the 1980s through the successful experiences of some countries such as Hong Kong, China, Japan, and Republic of Korea, which were able to increase their growth through ELG strategies, and not so successful experiences, mostly in Latin America, where import substituting polices did not yield the desired growth rates (Sach and Warner, 1995). ELG was proposed to generate higher capacity utilization and higher economies of scale, improve productivity and lead to better allocation of resources based on comparative advantage. A stream of empirical literature supported this ELG hypothesis (see Blecker [2000] for a comprehensive survey of the literature). The East Asian economic crisis of 1997 and the global economic crisis of the post-2007 period have shaken the belief in ELG strategies and have brought the role played by domestic demand in the forefront. It is argued that the domestic demand-based growth models can reduce dependency on other markets which may become volatile given the current economic scenario and it may provide cushion against the increasing competition given by Chinese exports in the third-country market (Felipe, 2003). One of the major criticisms against ELG strategies is that they lead to the creation of excess capacity in the manufacturing sector (Kaplinsky 1993; Ertuk, 1999). This excess capacity undermines the financial soundness of investments, as was the case for East Asian economies during the financial crisis. Some of the studies have further questioned the causality of this approach. According to Rodriguez and Rodrik (2000), successful export performance can be a result of successful development rather than the cause.

Along with ELG strategies, import Liberalization has also been proposed as a key to economic growth. Endogenous growth models have emphasised static as well as dynamic gains arising from imports (Romer 1987, 1990). Imports of intermediate products can enable the creation of new domestic varieties and further boost productivity (Grossman and Helpman, 1991; Kasahara and Rodrigue, 2008). It is argued that imports of consumer durables can lead to increase in domestic competition leading to improved productivity, while imports of improved technologies and capital goods can further foster higher efficiency and productivity gains. However, with higher imports there is also a danger of crowding out of domestic investments if the domestic industry is unable to compete. This may lead to reduced output and adversely affect productivity growth. In the case of India, in the post-1990 period, exports and imports of manufactures have grown steadily, with imports growing at a much faster rate than exports (Fig. 9). At current prices, the ratio of exports to manufacturing output increased from 10 per cent in 1980–81 to around 25 per cent in 2008–09 (Fig. 7). At real prices, the ratio was around 16 per cent in 2008–09.

Table 8	Average annual growth rate in real exports, real imports, and real value added in manufacturing and per capita income			
	Growth in real exports	Growth in real imports	Growth in real value added in organised manufacturing sector	Growth in real per capita income
1970s	7.5	1.9	4.1	1.4
1980s	7.0	4.2	8.0	3.2
1990s	10.7	13.3	5.9	3.6
2000–09	10.2	21.0	7.8	5.4

Source: Directorate General of Commercial Intelligence and Statistics (RBI – Handbook of Statistics).
Note: Growth rates for each year are arrived at by taking natural logs and then difference from the subsequent year. For manufacturing value added, the period is 2000–08.

Figure 7 Manufactures exports and imports as a percentage of organised manufacturing utput at current prices

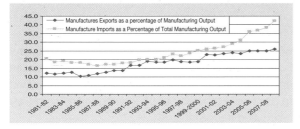

Source: Figures for manufacturing output is taken from Annual Survey of Industries and exports and imports form Reserve Bank of India. All figures are in crore at current prices.

In the post-1990 period, along with the surge in exports and imports, manufacturing sector also experienced a much higher average annual growth rate (Table 8). Although these trends suggest that trade may have led to this growth, it is important to note that along with trade, domestic economy also experienced its highest ever per annum growth in this decade. A rise in growth of real per capita income from 3.2 per cent in the 1980s to 3.6 per cent in the 1990s and further to 5.6 per cent in the 2000s highlights the growth in domestic demand and corresponding purchasing power.

Given this economic setting, the evident question which draws attention is the direction of causality in the relationship between growth in exports and imports with growth in manufacturing sector and the role played by rising domestic demand.

With respect to the Indian manufacturing sector, the impact of Liberalization on growth has been explained in terms of estimating productivity growth in pre- and post-Liberalization periods. Different methodologies have been used to arrive at productivity estimates. However, few studies have attempted to estimate the long-term and short-term relationships and causality of export/import growth and growth in the manufacturing sector. We use the co-integration analysis for identifying the long-term and short-term relationships and causality between export/import growths with growth in the manufacturing sector. Such an approach has been extensively used in the literature for testing the growth linkages between overall GDP growth and export growth to test ELG.

Studies using this approach for testing ELG hypothesis for the aggregate economy have arrived at mixed results. Numerous empirical studies (e.g. Thorton, 1996; Ekanayake 1999; Panas and Vamvoukas, 2002) find strong support for the ELG hypothesis. However, equally large number of studies are unable to support the ELG hypothesis for the economy as a whole (e.g. Rehman and Mustafa, 1997; Love and Chandra, 2005). Jung and Marshall (1985), for instance, using standard Granger causality tests, analysed the relationship between export growth and economic growth using time series data for 37 developing countries and found evidence for the export-led growth hypothesis in only four countries. Literature has generated more debate than consensus on this issue. In contrast to the export-led growth hypothesis, neoclassical trade theories typically stress that the causality runs from home-factor endowments and productivity to the supply of exports (e.g. Findlay, 1984).

ELG for India has been tested using time series analysis for the aggregate economy by some studies, including Dhawan and Biswal (1999), Ghatak and Price (1997), Krishan *et al.* (2008) and Pradhan (2010). For the Indian manufacturing sector, very limited studies exist which test for ELG hypothesis by testing for causality. Given the growing importance of services sector in terms of contribution to GDP growth and export growth, analysis at the aggregate economy level may not apply to the manufacturing sector. We undertake the multivariate co-integration analysis for the organised manufacturing sector using two specifications. First, we build a five-variable VAR model using the augmented production function approach, which has been widely used in this literature (Balassa 1978, Ram 1987, Greenway and Sapsford, 1994).

In the augmented production function approach, which goes beyond the traditional neoclassical theory of production, real output is taken as a function of labour, capital stock, real exports and real imports.[18] The inclusion of exports as an additional input provides an alternative to capture total factor productivity (TFP) growth, where it is assumed that total factor productivity can be rewritten as a function of exports (Xt), imports (Mt) and other exogenous factors (Ct) uncorrelated with Xt and Mt. Some studies have argued that it is necessary to separate the economic influence of exports on output from the influence incorporated into the growth accounting relationship (Islam, 1998). We address this issue by testing both aggregate output and aggregate output net of exports. Output net of exports provides a different interpretation as it would represent output produced for the domestic market. Relationship of exports to "output net of exports" provides insights into the extent of domestic linkages and spill-overs from the exportable sector to the rest of the manufacturing sector (Blecker, 2006). The analysis is undertaken for organised manufacturing sector from 1981–82 to 2008–09. Second, for testing the ELG hypothesis, growth in organised manufacturing GDP is taken as a function of growth of domestic demand and growth of external demand. This framework for explaining manufacturing growth was first used by Lawrence (1984). Subsequently, this was used by many studies (e.g. Lee and Cole, 1994). Growth in domestic demand is captured by growth in per capita GDP and real imports, while growth in external demand is captured through growth in real exports. The analysis is undertaken for the organised manufacturing sector from 1970–71 to 2009–10.

For testing these specifications data on output, employment and capital stock is taken from Annual Survey of Industries from 1981–82 to 2008–09.[19] The EPWRF (2007) database has been used which has been extended for remaining years with data collected directly from the CSO, ensuring that the two series match. Wholesale Price index deflators for manufactures are used to arrive at the constant price series (1993–94 prices). The capital stock has been represented by the net fixed capital (at constant price) using perpetual inventory method and implicit price deflators are used to deflate the series.[20] Exports and imports of manufactures have been estimated using data provided by the Reserve Bank of India (*Handbook of Statistics*). Export unit value index (1978–79 as base) and import unit value index have been used to arrive at real exports and real import series. Total persons engaged are used as employment in organised manufacturing sector. The per capita remuneration in each industry was derived from the ASI data and applied to this series. Manufacturing GDP and per capita GDP at constant prices of 1999–2000 are taken from the Central Statistical Organization. To determine the relationship between output growth and growth of exports and imports, we perform Johansen and Juselius (1990) Multivariate Cointegration test. To determine whether the series are stationary, Augmented Dickey-Fuller test and Phillips–Perron test are used. Johansen and Juselius Cointegration Test procedures are used to determine the number of co-integration vectors by estimating trace statistics.

The VECM estimated takes the following form:

$$\Delta LNY_t = c_0 + \sum_{i=1}^{n} [\alpha_i \Delta LK_{t-1} + \beta_i \Delta LL_{t-1} + \delta_i \Delta LM_{t-1} + \gamma_i \Delta LX_{t-1} + \varpi_i \Delta LNY_{t-1}] + \varphi_i ECT_t + u_t$$

$$\Delta LX_t = c_0 + \sum_{i=1}^{n} [\alpha_i \Delta LK_{t-1} + \beta_i \Delta LL_{t-1} + \delta_i \Delta LM_{t-1} + \gamma_i \Delta LX_{t-1} + \varpi_i \Delta LNY_{t-1}] + \phi_i ECT_t + e_t$$

where Δ is the difference operator, LN are natural logs, Y is manufacturing real output, K is net fixed capital stock in manufacturing sector, M is real imports of manufactures, X is real exports of manufactures, L is employment in organised manufacturing sector, and the ECT is the error correction term which represents the lagged error from the co-integration equation. Since we have relatively small number of observations to test this hypothesis, we use K/L ratio, i.e. capital intensity of labour in place of capital stock and labour.

The results of stationarity tests show that all series, real output, real output net of exports, real imports and real capital-labour ratio are found to be non-stationary in levels and stationary at first difference, which means that they are integrated at an of order of 1, so they are I (1) series. They, therefore, have a stochastic trend. In addition, the first difference of all the series rejects the unit root hypothesis implying that they become stationary at the first difference. Vector error correction models (VECM) mix levels and first differences to estimate the short run and long run simultaneously. Using one lag we arrive at the results of Johansen tests for co-integration using output and output net of exports. The results of the test show that there exist two co-integrating vectors, i.e. null hypothesis of no con-integration can be rejected at the 5 per cent significance level for both the equations using real output and real output net of exports. The results show that there exists long-term relationship between the variables.

The coefficients of error correction term are found to be negative and significant for the both the equations with real output and real output net of exports as the dependent variable. This indicates that any short-term fluctuations between the dependent and independent variables will lead to a stable long-term relationship.[21] Table 9 reports the co-integrating equations with respect to output and output net of exports. The results show that in the long run in both cases, exports do not have significant coefficient implying that exports in the long term may not have a significant impact on output, while imports have a significant impact on output. Capital labour ratio also has a significant impact in both cases.

To test the causality of relationships, we undertake Granger non-causality tests reporting Wald statistics based on the estimates of VAR model. A variable X Granger-causes Y if Y can be better predicted using the histories of both X and Y than it can by using the history of Y alone. Results of the Granger non-causality tests reported in Table 10, which show that the hypothesis that "exports do not Granger cause output" is accepted as test statistics is not found to be significant, while the hypothesis that "output does not cause exports" is rejected. This implies that the relationship between output growth and export growth runs from "output growth to export growth" and not the other way around. Higher growth in manufacturing output leads to higher exports. It is also found that higher growth of domestic output or "output net of exports" also Granger causes higher exports (Table 10). This can be the case if more and more firms explore international markets with growth of their output. The growing diversity of export basket may be the result of this output growth. Sharma and Panagiotidis (2005) arrived at similar results for aggregate Indian economy for 1971–2001. Short-term causality between imports and growth in output is found to be one way, higher imports Granger cause higher output but higher output does not necessarily Granger cause higher imports. This is an interesting result as it also indicates that output for domestic market may not be too dependent on imports in the short term. More interesting are the results relating to causality between exports and imports. Results for "output net of exports" show that there exists, two-way relationships between exports and imports. Higher exports lead to higher imports and higher imports also lead to higher exports in the short term.

The result that exports does not affect growth of manufacturing "output net of exports" but is affected by imports can be interpreted as lack of domestic linkages of exportables with domestic output (Blecker, 2006). Higher exports can lead to higher total manufacturing output if the import content of exports is low. Some studies found a negative impact of exports on domestic output, e.g. in case of Mexico. Moreno-Brid et al. (2005) found that around 70 per cent of Mexico's exports of manufactures are produced through assembly processes involving imported inputs that enter the country under preferential tax schemes, which allows tax-free entry of imported inputs and raw materials for export purposes. This has led to reduction in local content in Mexico's manufactured exports and weak linkages of exports with domestic suppliers. Blecker (2006) also find a similar result for Mexico and concludes that the more Mexico integrates into the global value chains, the less it integrates with the domestic economy.

Table 9	Results of co-integrating equations			
	LN K/L	LN EXP	LNIMP	Constant
_ce1 real LN output				
coefficient	0.42***	0.19	0.35***	2.75
Std Err	0.086	0.12	0.10	
Z	5.33	1.63	3.33	
P	0.00	0.13	0.001	
_ce1 real LN output net of exports				
coefficient	0.53***	0.21	0.43**	1.13
Std Err	0.15	0.20	0.17	
z	3.59	1.03	2.52	
P	0.00	0.30	0.01	

Table 10   Results of Granger non-causality tests between real output, real output net of exports, real exports and real imports

Dependent variables	Independent variables	Chi2	Causality
Output growth	Export growth	0.13	Growth in real exports does not Granger causes growth in real output
	Import growth	26.4***	Growth in real imports Granger causes growth in real output
Export growth	Output growth	1.66***	Growth in real output Granger causes growth in real exports
	Import growth	0.003	Growth in real imports does not Granger cause growth in real exports
Import growth	Output growth	1.49	Growth in real output does not Granger cause growth in real imports
	Export growth	2.11	Growth in real exports does not Granger cause growth in real imports
Growth in output net of exports	Export growth	3.86	Growth in real exports does not Granger cause growth in real output net of exports
	Import growth	9.25*	Growth in real imports Granger causes growth in real output net of exports
Export growth	Growth in output net of exports	8.05**	Growth in real output net of exports Granger causes growth in real exports
	Import growth	10.21**	Growth in real imports Granger causes growth in real output net of exports
Import growth	Growth in output net of exports	5.03	Growth in real output net of exports does not Granger cause growth in real imports
	Export growth	9.44**	Growth in real exports Granger causes growth in real imports
Growth in output	Growth in per capita income	12.35***	Growth in per capita income Granger causes growth in real output
Growth in per capita income	Growth in output	19.4	Growth in real output Granger causes growth in per capita income

Lack of evidence of growth of manufacturing exports affecting growth of manufacturing "output net of exports" in the long term in case of India implies that growth in Indian manufacturing in the 2000s has not really been an export-led growth and may not be led by export growth in the future. This result is corroborated by the results arrived at by other studies for India which have estimated long-term relationship between export growth and total GDP growth by estimating VECM. Asafu-Adjaye *et al.* (1999) consider three variables: exports, real output and imports for 1960–94. They do not find any evidence of the existence of a causal relationship between these variables in case of India and no support for the ELG hypothesis. Using similar methodology for 1961–92, Dhawan and Biswal (1999) also find no long-term relationship. Chandra (2002) fails to find any support for long-run relationship between real exports and real GDP. Ghatak and Price (1997) use "GDP net of exports" as regressor,

along with exports and imports as additional variables to test the ELG hypothesis for India during 1960–92, Their results indicate that real export growth was Granger-caused by non-export real GDP growth over 1960–92. Their co-integration tests confirm the long-run nature of this relationship.

Imports of manufactures, on the other hand, are found to have a long-term impact on growth of manufacturing output net of exports. Imports of manufactures comprise imports of industrial supplies, capital goods, consumer durables and other manufactures. In India, tariff Liberalization has been faster for capital goods and industrial intermediate goods or industrial supplies. In the 2000s, tariffs fell drastically even for consumer durables. Higher imports of technology via capital goods and better quality inputs impact productivity and efficiency growth and lead to a positive impact on manufacturing output growth. Imports of consumer durables increase domestic competition and may further add to improvements in productivity and efficiency leading to higher output growth in the manufacturing sector. A similar relationship with respect to imports and output and productivity growth in India is found by other studies such as Rodrik (1995), Goldberg et al. (2009) and Topalova and Khandelwal (2010). To confirm this result a different specification has also been attempted for the manufacturing sector using a longer time series (1970–2009). Total manufacturing GDP is taken as a function of domestic demand and external demand. Growth in domestic demand is captured by growth in per capita income and real imports, while growth in external demand is captured by growth in exports.

Growth in Registered Manufacturing GDP = f (Growth in Domestic Demand for manufactures and Growth in External Demand for manufactures)

The results of this specification do not differ qualitatively from the above results.[22] The Granger causality results (Table 10) show that domestic demand in terms of growth of per capita income has a significant impact on the growth of total manufacturing sector, while growth in exports does not lead to growth in manufacturing sector in the long term. Short-term results arrived at by VECM model indicate that imports with a lag are found to impact manufacturing output in period t and higher per capita income with two lags impacts manufacturing output. Exports even with two lags do not have any significant impact. With the slowdown of the global economy in the post-economic crisis of 2007, one of the major concerns has been the impact of slowdown in external demand on the growth of the Indian manufacturing sector. Results suggest that the jump in the growth of manufacturing sector in the last decade can be explained more by growth in domestic demand and imports rather than growth in exports. The results also show that exports in India are dependent on imports.

One of the plausible reasons why exports may not be playing a leading role in the growth of the Indian manufacturing sector is that even with rising growth of exports, the total share of exports in manufacturing output is still small at around 25 per cent at current prices and not more than 16 per cent in real terms, showing that major part of the output still caters to the domestic market. Higher growth of imports adds to the manufacturing growth in many different ways, i.e. through increase in productivity and efficiency due to imported technology and better quality of imported inputs and through providing competition in the do-

mestic market which encourages domestic firms to improve their quality, pricing and efficiency of delivery for preserving their market share from imported products.

E. Success Stories within Manufacturing Sector

The results with respect to structural breaks and co-integration analysis indicate that growth of exports did not play a major role in the manufacturing sector's growth. However, imports played an important role in boosting manufacturing output growth as well as export growth. Examining industrial growth rates provide a more disaggregated picture with respect to industries and may help identify success stories of industries in the manufacturing sector which experienced higher growth in the 2000s. It needs to be examined whether these were also the industries where exports and/or imports played a comparatively greater role incentivised by trade policy.

The average annual growth of value addition at the sector level shows that more than 10 per cent average annual growth from 2000–01 to 2007–08 occurred, apart from petroleum products sector, in motor vehicles, trailers and semi-trailers; fabricated metal products; wood and wood products; furniture and other manufacturing; leather and leather products; office, accounting and computing machinery; electrical machinery; other transport equipment; food products and beverages; and medical precision and optical instruments (Table 11). Out of the these, top five industries with respect to change in average annual growth in value addition in 2000s over the 1990s were wood and wood products, petroleum products, medical precision and optical instruments, publishing, printing and related activities, office accounting and computing machinery and paper and paper products (Table 11).

However, these industries do not figure in the list of top five industries with highest contribution to manufacturing exports, apart from petroleum products. 85 per cent of manufacturing exports take place from 13 broad industries and four out of the top five industries which reported higher change in the growth of value addition do not appear in the list of the industries with relatively higher contribution to manufactures exports (Table 3). Domestic demand seems to have played a much more important role than external demand in their growth. Kumari (2010) also found similar results:

Contribution of domestic demand in output growth was higher than the growth of external demand in the post-Liberalization period. Interestingly, the top three industries where the contribution of exports to total exports has increased the most, i.e. non-metallic mineral products, chemical and chemical products and basic metals (Table 4), the average annual growth in value addition in all the four industries has declined from 2000–01 to 2008–09 compared with the 1990s, while their contribution to total imports has increased in 2009 compared with 2000.

Table 12 reports decadal average annual growth rates in value added of broad industrial categories along with contribution of these industries to total exports and imports of manufacturing sector. Simple average tariffs over the decades are also reported. Table 11 shows that the sectors with double-digit average annual growth rates of value added in the 1990s were motor vehicles, electrical machinery, fabricated metal products and petroleum products. These industries continued to grow at double-digit rate from 2000–01 to 2008–09. Out of these, industries which experi-

Table 11 Sectoral average annual growth in real value added in organised manufacturing sector (percentage)			
	AVG11980s	AVG191990s	AVG 2000s
Coke, petroleum products and nuclear fuel	-0.1	0.6	19.4
Motor vehicles, trailers and semi-trailers	6.9	14.8	16.5
Fabricated metal products	1.9	13.4	15.5
Wood and wood products	7.5	-13.5	14.8
Furniture and other manufacturing N.E.C.	4.1	29.7	13.0
Leather and related products	5.1	9.5	13.0
Office, accounting and computing machinery	4.8	5.8	12.8
Electrical machinery and apparatus, N.E.C	9.7	15.8	12.3
Other transport equipment	6.6	10.2	11.9
Food products and beverages	18.6	8.6	11.1
Medical, precision and optical instruments	11.6	0.7	10.5
Paper and paper products	3.1	4.3	9.8
Publishing, printing and related activities	-1.9	0.7	9.3
Wearing apparel, dressing and dyeing of fur	14.3	15.5	9.0
Textile products	4.9	12.8	8.0
Machinery and equipment N.E.C.	5.7	14.0	7.1
Non-metallic mineral products	8.6	9.5	7.1
Chemicals and chemical products	11.1	10.1	3.8
Basic metals	0.5	17.5	3.3
Radio, television and communication equipment	28.1	14.8	1.8
Tobacco and related products	1.7	7.7	-1.4
Rubber and plastic products	8.0	8.5	-2.0
Others	5.5	10.1	8.5
Total manufacturing	**6.5**	**11.5**	**8.7**

Note: Average annual growth rates of value added are calculated from Annual Survey of Industries. Double Deflation method is used. The 2000s comprise 2000–01 to 2008–09.

enced increase in their value added growth compared with the 1990s and also experienced higher export and import growth can be categorised as success stories. There are two such industries: motor vehicles, trailers and semi-trailers; electrical machinery and apparatus. Tariffs in these industries were lowered but they continued to remain high for motor vehicles. Food products and beverages experienced a rise in growth of value added and exports but fall in imports. This could be because of the rise in tariffs for this industry. Given the importance of this industry with respect to its backward linkages with the agriculture sector, higher growth in this industry with lower import growth qualifies this industry as a success story.

Rising imports in a sector along with rising exports but falling value added growth in that sector indicates that rise in exports over time is fuelled by rise in imports rather output growth in the manufacturing sector. This also indicates that the nature of import in these industries may be more of the intermediate goods compared with capital goods, which increase productivity and efficiency. The growing import content in exports has become an issue of concern in many developing countries. Industries which have witnessed a fall in their value added growth but rise in their export growth and import growth in 2000s compared with the 1990s are potential cases of increased import intensity of exports. These are chemicals and chemical products and basic metals. The double-digit value added growth in the 1990s was followed by less than 5 per cent growth in their value added. These industries need to be closely monitored for a possible "hollowing out" wherein the externalities of export growth spill to the external sector and the domestic economy is unable to reap the economies which arise because of higher exports. There has been a drastic fall in tariffs of these industries during the 2000s compared with 1990.

Some industries have witnessed a fall in their value added growth along with a fall in their export growth as well as import growth. They can be categorised as not so successful stories. These are wearing apparel, dressing and dyeing of fur, textile products; and non-metallic mineral products. The case of textiles and wearing apparels is a bit surprising. This sector enjoys a number of export incentives and has enjoyed high protection, but despite this, export growth has slowed down in the 2000s. An important reason for this could be the intense competitive pressure on prices on account of exports from China, Bangladesh, Mexico, etc. Another cause could be high protection and lower import growth of this sector.

Apart from domestic market growth, growth in imports has led to the sector's growth. This sector has been over-protected in terms of its imports of intermediate goods as well as final goods. These results have a strong connotation for Indian manufacturing sector in the post-2008 global crisis period. The results explain the puzzle regarding the manufacturing sector's growth and its exports despite slowdown in external demand. The growth is fuelled by the growing domestic demand for the manufactures as the per capita income rises. Higher domestic demand is plausibly creating growth in output and value added in industries which are not necessarily export oriented. This growth in the domestic market-oriented industries is also probably creating more demand for imports, especially for the capital goods and industrial intermediate goods. Demand for imported consumer durables is also rising with growth in incomes. Rising domestic competition and better imported technology and intermediate products are further fuelling the growth in the domestic-market oriented industries. However, in this growth-propelling process, export-oriented industries are being left out. This may be leading to the rising import content in their exports. This may have further adverse effects on their growth as their domestic linkages lower with rising import content and they are further isolated from the domestic growth.

F. Conclusions and Broad Lessons from Indian Experience

Much of the growth in India's GDP has been contributed by growth in services sector. However, India's manufacturing sector has also experienced its highest-ever average annual decadal growth in the 2000s, growing at an average annual growth rate of 8 per cent. This was accompanied by its highest-ever decadal growth in exports as well as imports (average annual growth rates of 11 and 27 per cent). The trade policy's role in the growth of the manufacturing sector is an issue of great importance, not only for India but also for other developing countries which have limited tools of development at their disposal. In this context, this chapter investigates the extent to which trade acted as a driver of growth in the manufacturing sector. In particular, using different methodologies we examine whether growth in Indian manufacturing was an export-led growth or an import-induced growth. We also attempt to assess the role of India's trade Liberalization policies in the growth of the manufacturing sector.

Table 12   Average annual growth in value added, contribution to exports and imports and tariffs

	Average annual growth rates of real value-added		Contribution to total manufacturing imports		Contribution to total manufacturing exports		Simple average tariffs		
	1990s	2000s	1990	2009	1990	2009	1996	2000	2008
High-growth industries									
Coke, petroleum products and nuclear fuel	0.6	19.4	3.1	14.8	27.3	34	20.6	8.1	6.73
Motor vehicles, trailers and semi-trailers	14.8	16.5	2.3	6.3	3.9	4.7	39.4	48.3	20.91
Electrical machinery and apparatus, N.E.C.	15.8	12.3	1.7	5.8	4.4	9.3	30.9	27.2	6.9
Fabricated metal products	13.4	15.5	2.1	1.8			25	30.4	9.92
Food products and beverages	8.6	11.1	9.2	3.4	1.1	2.8	54.2	37.7	41.19
Growth declines									
Non-metallic mineral products	9.5	7.1	16.8	11.4	9.1	6.8			9.08
Chemicals and chemical products	10.1	3.8	9.5	11.1	12.3	9.9	39.8	8.3	8.3
Basic metals	17.5	3.3	6.2	10.4	10.6	8.2	25.3	30.8	5.17
Wearing apparel, dressing and dyeing of fur	15.5	9	15.3	7.5			50.7	10	10
Textile products	12.8	8	16.2	6.5	2.1	1.3	50.1	9.4	9.8

India's trade Liberalization policy has changed face several times since the 1980s. The 1980s were more dominated by export promoting policies, while the 1990s and 2000s saw more emphasis on import Liberalization. Accordingly, the average annual growth of exports in the 1980s was much higher than that of imports in the 1980s, but in the 1990s and 2000s, the average annual growth of imports surpassed that of exports. In the 2000s, real imports grew at an average annual growth of 27 per cent compared with 10 per cent of real exports. However, India's import Liberalization differed considerably in its extent and spread from other developing countries. The import Liberalization policy followed by India can be described as cautious and sequential. Import duties on capital goods were lowered in mid-1980s, followed by lowering of import duties on raw materials and intermediate products in the 1990s and eventually import duties were lowered for consumer goods in 2001. However, standard deviation of tariffs within the industry increased in many industries in 2009 compared with 1990 reflecting that strategic protection which is still being followed in some industries. Some of these industries are motor vehicles and food product and beverages.

The chapter follows different methodologies and specifications to test the interlinkages between growth in exports, imports and manufacturing output. To assess the importance of trade reforms in the growth process of the manufacturing sector, two kinds of structural breaks are identified in the growth series of total manufacturing value added and output of organised sector. These are "gradual" structural break, which adds dynamically to future growth, and "instant" break, which shifts the growth trajectory. Gradual shifts are more important in identifying the effectiveness of policy changes as they add dynamically into the system. The results of AO and IO models show that for total manufacturing sector, the structural break that adds dynamically to the rest of the growth process came in 1991, while the sudden break points in growth came in 1997. The reforms of 1980s, which were more export oriented did not lead to any sudden shifts or gradual shifts in value added growth of total manufacturing sector. However, for the registered manufacturing sector, the results using double deflated value added series for the organised manufacturing (which is used by most studies estimating productivity growth) show that the sudden breaks are found in 1991 and 1998, while gradual shifts in the mean of the series came around 1986 and 2001.

This indicates that it is plausible that the reforms of 2000, which were more effective in dismantling of protection to the sector, led to a gradual shift in the growth of organised manufacturing sector, while the reforms of the 1990s, which were much broader in scope, led to a gradual shift in the growth trajectory of total manufacturing sector. The industrial policy of 1980s, which encouraged export-oriented production and import of technology, appears to have had a greater impact on the organised sector than on the unorganised sector. Significant structural breaks in export and import growths are found in 2001 and 2002. Tariff Liberalization gathered speed after 2001, when across-the-board tariffs in manufactures, especially consumer durables, were brought down to 10 per cent. This period also coincides with the policy of removal of quantitative restrictions on consumer durables and a spurt in imports of capital goods and machinery. Seen with the drastic changes in import Liberalization policies in this period, it can be asserted that these policies were effective. However, the industrial policy of export promotion of the 1980s does not seem to have played an important role in terms of causing a structural break in export growth, but policies such as the removal of some items, including garments, shoes, toys and auto components, from the small-scale reserved list in 2001 may have played some role.

The structural breaks in manufacturing growth and growth of exports and imports coincide around early 2000s indicating some causal relationship between trade and the manufacturing sector's growth. To estimate the long-term and short-term relationships between the growth of manufacturing output and the growth of exports and imports, we undertake multivariate co-integration analysis for the organised manufacturing sector using two specifications. First, we build a five-variable VAR model using the augmented production function approach. VECM is estimated with growth of "total manufacturing output" and "manufacturing output net of exports" is used as dependent variable for deeper insights. The other variables are real exports, real imports, real capital stock and labour. Second, based on growth accounting framework, output growth is taken as a function of growth in domestic demand, (captured by growth in per capita income and growth in imports) and growth in external demand captured by growth in exports.

The results based on both the specifications are qualitatively similar. They reveal that the Indian manufactur-

ing sector's growth is not an export-led growth but an import-Induced growth. Growth in exports does not seem to have contributed to growth in total manufacturing output in the long term, and the causality runs from growth in output to growth in exports. Short-term results with respect to causality also show that in the short-term export growth does not seem to cause growth in output. Interestingly, causality from export growth to growth in output net of exports is also not found. This can be interpreted as exports having lower linkages with the domestic sector as it does not affect the growth of the output produced for the domestic economy. Import growth, on the other hand, according to the estimated results, have Granger caused output growth as well as export growth. This indicates export growth is driven by imports rather than domestic production. This can be an area of concern for the economy as the potential advantages of a robust export growth spills to the external sector rather than being used internally by the domestic industry. The analysis at the aggregate level is substantiated by sectoral analysis. Interestingly, industries which have experienced increase in their contribution to total exports of manufacturing sector in the 2000s compared with the 1990s have also witnessed a slowdown in the average annual growth rates in the 2000s compared with the 1990s. The top five industries where growth has improved in the 2000s compared with the 1990s – wood and wood products, medical precision and optical instruments, publishing, printing and related activities, office accounting and computing machinery and paper and paper products – are not export oriented.

The success stories at the sector level include industries which have experienced higher value added growth in the last decade than in the 1990s and have also experienced higher export and import growth in this period. There are two such industries: motor vehicles, trailers and semi-trailers; food and food products. However, there are some not-so-successful stories which have witnessed a fall in their value added growth along with a fall in their export growth as well as import growth. These are wearing apparels, dressing and dyeing of fur; textile products; and non-metallic mineral products. The case of textiles and wearing apparels is a bit surprising. This sector enjoys a number of export incentives, but despite this, export growth has slowed down in the 2000s along with its value added growth. One apparent cause could be slowdown in external demand, but that could have been overcome by the domestic market as in the case of other consumer exportable. Another cause could be high protection and lower import growth to this sector. Some more worrisome cases are industries which have experienced a fall in their value added growth in the 2000s compared with the 1990s but a rise in their export growth as well as import growth. These industries are electrical machinery and apparatus, N.E.C; chemicals and chemical products; basic metals; and machinery and equipment nec. These industries need to be closely monitored for a possible "hollowing out" wherein the externalities of export growth spill to the external sector and the domestic sector is unable to reap the economies which arise due to higher exports. This is now one of the major challenges facing Indian trade policymakers.

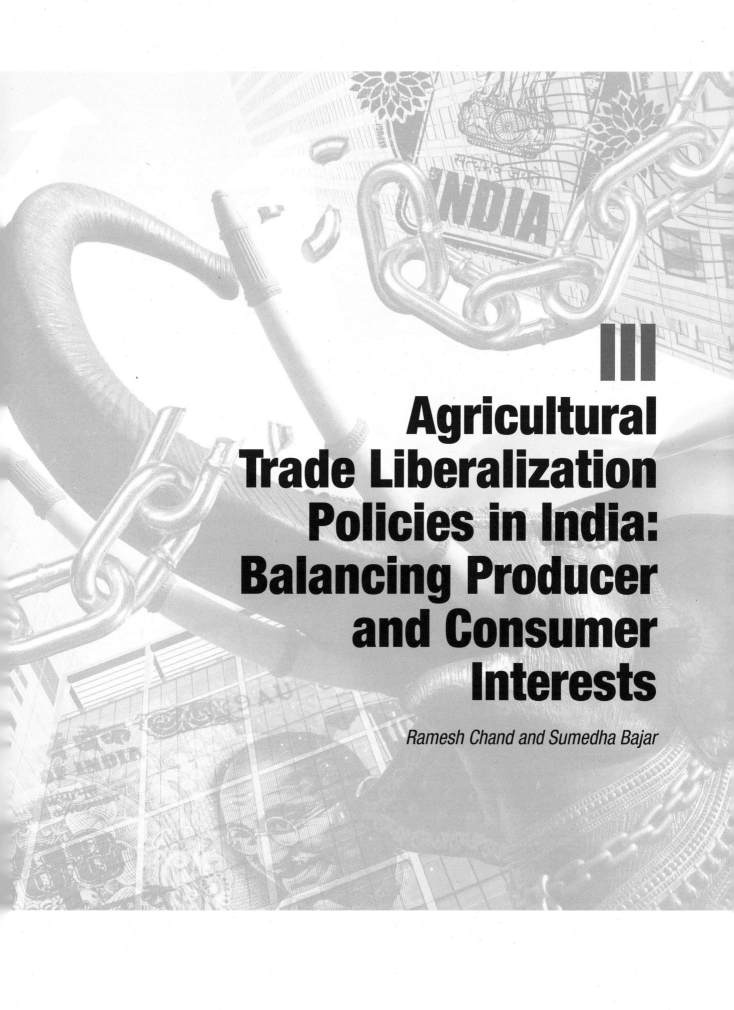

III
Agricultural Trade Liberalization Policies in India: Balancing Producer and Consumer Interests

Ramesh Chand and Sumedha Bajar

A. Introduction

India followed an inward-looking and highly protectionist trade policy in agriculture till early 1990s. Barring a few traditional commercial commodities, agricultural trade was subjected to measures like quantitative restrictions, canalization, licenses, quotas and high tariff rates. These measures strictly regulated imports and exports to safeguard domestic producers' and consumers' interests. In most commodities levels of export and import were determined by fluctuations in domestic supply and exports were residuals. Similarly, imports were allowed with fall in domestic production to fill the gap between domestic demand and supply. The production pattern was strictly guided by domestic requirement and self sufficiency in almost all major commodities. Allocation of resources based on comparative advantage in trade did not get much emphasis. This scenario started changing with economic reforms of 1991. External trade was further liberalised with the implementation of WTO Agreement on Agriculture in 1995. The process was accelerated after India lost the dispute in WTO to retain Quantitative Restrictions (QRs) on ground of Balance of Payment

Soon after economic reforms began in 1991, followed by the new export-import policy[23] announced on 31 March 1992 to speed up trade Liberalization, serious debate commenced on the impact of trade openness on agriculture. It was argued that since 1947, India had protected its industrial sector through trade policy by insulating it from foreign markets and disprotected its agriculture (Rao and Gulati, 1994; Singh, 1995; Gulati and Sharma, 1995). As economic reforms and trade Liberalization involved reduced protection to the domestic industry and downward adjustment in overvalued exchange rate, they were expected to improve terms of trade and export prospects for the agriculture sector. These two changes have reportedly resulted in significant reduction in the anti-agriculture bias through more balanced degree of relative sectoral protection (Dholkia, 1997).

The more intense debate on the impact of trade Liberalization and increase in openness on agriculture started after WTO came into being in 1995, even though India had liberalised agriculture trade partly for WTO commitments and partly for domestic policy considerations. This debate has covered several issues. Some scholars feel there are tremendous opportunities for Indian agriculture to benefit from increased openness and benefit from trade by reallocation of resources based on the principle of comparative advantage (Gulati and Sharma 1994, Gulati and Kohli 1996, Gulati and Sharma 1997, Gulati 2001, 2002, Pursel and Gulati 1995, Parikh et al. 1995, 1997). Therefore, this school of thought emphasises closer integration of Indian agriculture with world agriculture and favours openness. The other group of scholars is sceptical about gains from international trade in agriculture for several reasons (Storm 1997, 2001; Bhalla 2004, Nayyar and Sen, 1994a and 1994b; Chand 1999; Chand and Jha 2001; Chand 2002a and 2002b), especially two main reasons. First, international prices are highly distorted and do not represent true opportunity cost of resources. Second, world prices suffer from serious year-to-year fluctuations, and free trade will transmit volatility to domestic prices, which is not considered favourable to consumers and producers in developing countries. This school of thought believes India should follow strategic openness rather than general or indiscriminate openness in agriculture. Further, according to the first school of thought, trade offers a better option for stabilising domestic supply and prices than stabilization through costly buffer stock operations (Jha and Srinivasan, 1999), whereas the second school of thought favours stocks and domestic stabilization (Chand, 2003).

The issue of self-sufficiency in food production in India has also received considerable attention. On the one hand, it has been argued that a large country cannot rely on the global market for its food requirements as international supply is limited and global prices are very sensitive to export/import decision of a country like India. On the other hand, merits of self-reliance as against self-sufficiency have also been highlighted (Gulati and Kohli, 1996). There have been concerns about implications of openness for food security and livelihood, as a large segment of population depends heavily on agriculture. A balanced view was put forward by Chakravarty and Singh (1988), before India embraced the opening up of its economy. According to them, there is no unique optimum level of economic openness for all countries at all times. Wrong kind of openness and/or the timing and sequence of openness could cause irreversible losses.

Empirical evidence on effects of trade Liberalization in agriculture based on the computable general equilibrium (CGE) model is sharply divided. Storm (2001) demonstrates that the cost of close integration of India's agriculture sector with the world economy is large and also unequally distributed. Results suggest that quantitative restrictions (QRs) on trade or varying levies on export and import may be desirable. Storm also argues that while close integration leads to a large fall in GDP growth and a dramatic decline in low-income households' real income, strategic integration results in significant rise in real GDP and a considerable improvement in the income of low-income classes. The paper underscores that regulated trade, rather than Liberalization, plays an effective role in domestic price policy. In contrast, Parikh et al. (1995, 1997) and Panda and Quizon (2001) found that in the short run, trade Liberalization adversely affects both growth and equity. In the medium and long run, trade Liberalization was found to accelerate growth by inducing more efficient resource allocation across sectors – and in the process helped reduce poverty. Both set of studies use base scenarios which reflect given situation, and their conclusions seem relevant if that scenario holds. However, international price situation is highly volatile and the ratio of domestic to international prices shows wide swings. Thus, benefits from trade do not always follow the same pattern. In some cases, the trade scenario shifts from export surplus to import dependence. This completely changes the trade equation and estimates of gain from trade. Therefore, it is important to look at the effects of openness on producers, consumers and various economic aspects over a period of time taking into account different phases of volatility in international prices rather than making a conclusion just by comparing limited periods.

It has now been almost two decades since India embraced economic openness as a part of the new economic policy. Global Liberalization under the WTO has also completed one and a half decade. This is sufficiently long period to understand implications of economic openness involving Liberalization and integration of the domestic economy with the global economy on Indian agriculture. Obviously, trade Liberalization affects producers and consumers differently. In simple terms, Liberalization of exports that results in increased domestic prices is favourable to producers. However, it affects consumers adversely as domestic prices and consumer expenditure rise and demand is reduced. Conversely, import Liberalization that results in lowered domestic prices is favourable to consumers but adversely affects producers, who get lower price for their produce. Many countries face serious difficulties in balancing producers' and consumers' interests in their trade policy. India, too, faces this policy conflict in most agricultural commodities. For any single agri-

cultural commodity, the country has a very large number of producers and also a large number of consumers. This chapter discusses and discerns how India has balanced producers' and consumers' interests, following the progressive Liberalization of trade after economic reforms started in 1991.

B. Trade Policy Changes Since 1991

The main objectives of agro-food trade policy before the initiation of economic reforms in 1991 were import substitution and self-sufficiency. Agro-food imports and exports were strictly regulated. The level of export and import of most commodities was determined by fluctuations in domestic supply, and exports were residuals. Similarly, imports were allowed to fill the gap between domestic demand and supply following a fall in domestic production. There was little emphasis on export-oriented production, and the production pattern of all major commodities was strictly guided by requirements of domestic consumers and self-sufficiency. Allocation of resources according to comparative advantage in trade hardly got any emphasis. Trade policy for agriculture was highly protective and inward looking. Except for a few traditional commercial commodities, agricultural trade was subjected to measures such as QRs, canalization, licenses, quotas and high tariff rates.

This scenario witnessed significant changes after 1991, when India started economic reforms and adopted a new economic policy. Under the new policy, rupee was devalued by 18 per cent against the dollar and the exchange rate was left to be determined by market forces. Following this, new initiatives in trade policy were undertaken to provide a stimulus to exports while at the same time reducing the degree of regulation and licensing control on foreign trade. The scope of canalization for both exports and imports was narrowed. These policy changes aimed to strengthen export incentives, eliminate import licensing and optimise import compression. The full expression of new trade measures was seen in the Export-Import Policy announced on 31 March 1992. The Export-Import Policy for 1992/1997 was announced for five years instead of three, as in the past. The main features of the policy were that trade was free except for a small negative lists of imports and exports. Imports of 3 items was banned, 80 items restricted, and 8 items canalised. These and various other changes in trade policy during 1991–2011 are presented in tables 1 and 2.

Table 1	Changes in Export Policy for selected agricultural commodities during 1992–2011			
Commodity	**Commodities covered in different periods**			
	1992–97	**1997–2002**	**2004–09**	**2007–11**
Wheat	Free, subject to QC and MEP	Free s.t. QC	Free	Ban,
Rice	Free s.t. QLs and MEP	Free	Free	lifted in 2011
Maize for feed	Free	Free	Free	Ban,
Maize	Free s.t. QC and MEP	Free s.t. QC	Free	relaxed/lifted in 2011
Rapeseed /mustard	Restricted	Free	Free	
Soybean	Restricted	Free	Free	
Groundnut	Restricted, except H.P.S. which is free	Free	Free	
Milk	Restricted	Restricted	Free	
Poultry meat	Free	Free	Free	
Sheep meat	Free	Free	Free	
Eggs	Free	Free	Free	
Cotton	Regulated	Free	Free	
Sugar	Free s.t. QC	Free s.t. QC	Free	
Coffee	Free	Free	Free	
Tea	Free	Free	Free	

Source: 1. Export-Import Policy, 1992–97, Government of India, New Delhi.
2. Export-Import Policy, 1997–2002, Government of India, New Delhi.
3. Export-Import Policy, 2004–09, Government of India, New Delhi.

Table 2	Changes announced in import policy for selected agricultural commodities during 1992–2009		
Commodity	**1992–97**	**1997–2002**	**2004–09**
Wheat, rice, maize	Canalised	Canalised till 1999, then freed. Again canalised from 2002	Canalised/free
Maize for feed	Free, for poultry units	Free, for poultry units	Free, for poultry units
Rapeseed-mustard seed, soybean seed, groundnut seed	Canalised	Canalised till1999. Then freed	Free
Milk	Skimmed milk free, whole milk restricted	Skimmed milk free, whole milk restricted	Free
Poultry meat	Restricted	Restricted	Free
Sheep meat	Restricted	Restricted	Free
Eggs	Restricted	Restricted	Restricted
Cotton	Restricted	Free	Free
Sugar	Free	Free	Free
Tea	Restricted	Restricted	Free
Coffee	Restricted	Restricted	Free

Source: Same as in Table 1.

The policy aimed at simplification and transparency. Procedural formalities were significantly reduced. The new policy was the most liberal trade policy regime implemented by India since 1947. In the very first year of its implementation, a number of initiatives were taken. These included (i) liberalised exchange rate management system; (ii) Liberalization of import licensing; (iii) export promotion capital goods scheme under which the import of capital goods was permitted at a concessional import duty; (iv) extension of export-oriented units and export-processing zone schemes to agriculture, horticulture, poultry, and animal husbandry; (v) tariff rationalization; (vi) adequate export credit at low interest rate and (vii) measures to encourage foreign investments. Until 1992, agricultural exports and imports in the country were strictly regulated through QRs such as quotas and licenses or channelled through some trading organization or some combination of both. In the Exim policy an-

nounced in 1992, three major changes were made in agricultural trade. One, channelling of trade was abandoned and government stopped determining the value or nature of import or exports, except for export of onion and import of cereals, pulses and edible oils. Two, most QRs on agricultural trade flows were removed. Three, there was some reduction in the tariff (Table 3).

Regarding agriculture, the stated objective of this trade policy was to enhance export capabilities of the agriculture sector by promoting productivity, modernization and competitiveness. The benefits available under the scheme of 100 per cent export-oriented unit and export-processing zones were extended to agriculture and allied sectors.

After five years, the next Exim Policy for the period 1 April 1997 to 31 March 2002 was released. The principal objectives of this policy were

Table 3   Import tariff and bound rate on agricultural commodities

Commodity	1990–91 and 1991–92	1993–94	1994–95	1995–96	1996–2000	2000–01	2001–02	2003–04	2009–10	Bound tariff
Rice (non-basmati)	0	0	0	0	0	92	77	70–80	80	70
Wheat	0	0	0	0	0	108	100	100	Free	100
Maize	0	0	0	0	0	60	50	50	50	70
Soya bean	60	85	65	50	50	35	35	30	30	45
Rapeseed/ mustard	60	85	65	50	50	35	35	30	30	100
Groundnut	60	85	65	50	50	35	35	30	30	100
Sugar	35	85	65	0	50	100	60		60	150
Tea	100	10	10	10	10	15	70	100	100	150
Coffee	100	10	10	10	10	15	70	100	100	100
Milk	60	85	40	50	0	30	35	30	30	100
Sheep meat	100	10	10	10	10	35	35	30	30	100
Eggs	100	85	65	40	30	35	35	30	30	100
Cotton	35	45	65	50	45	35	5	30	30	Unbnd
Palm oil, Groundnut, sunflower, coconut oil						100	85	75/85 85/100	Free/ 7.5	300
Rapeseed oil						75	75	75	Free	75
Pulses	10	10	10	10	10	5	5	10	Free	100
Onion	100	10	10	10	10	10	10	5	5	100

Source: Agricultural Statistics at a Glance, Ministry of Agriculture, GOI, various issues.

(1) To accelerate the country's transition to a globally oriented vibrant economy to derive maximum benefits from expanding global market opportunities

(2) To stimulate sustained economic growth by providing access to raw materials, intermediaries, components, consumables and capital goods required for augmenting production

(3) To enhance the technological strength and efficiency of agriculture, industry and services, thereby improving competitive strength while generating new employment opportunities, and encourage the attainment of international standards of quality

(4) To provide consumers with good-quality products at reasonable prices

Further changes were introduced in the Exim policy announced in August 2004 for 2004–09. This policy was a significant departure from the past, since it recognised trade as a means of economic growth and national development. The policy had the following two major objectives:

1. To double India's percentage share of global merchandise trade within the next five years
2. To act as an effective instrument of economic growth by giving a thrust to employment generation

These objectives were proposed to be achieved by adopting, among others, the following strategies:

    i. Unshackling of controls
    ii. Creating an atmosphere of trust and transparency
    iii. Simplifying procedures and bringing down transaction costs
    iv. Adopting the fundamental principle that duties and levies should not be exported
    v. Facilitating India's development as a global hub for manufacturing, trading and services.
    vi. Identifying and nurturing special focus areas which would generate additional employment opportunities, particularly in semi-urban and rural areas, and developing a series of "Initiatives" for each of these
    vii. Avoiding inverted duty structures and ensuring that India's domestic sectors are not disadvantaged in the Free Trade Agreements/Regional Trade Agreements/Preferential Trade Agreements that the country enters into in order to enhance its exports

The Exim Policy 2004–09 was projected as a road map for the development of India's foreign trade. Under the Special Focus Initiative, there was a package for agriculture, which included

a. Vishesh Krishi Upaj Yojana (Special Agricultural Produce Scheme), a scheme introduced to boost exports of fruits, vegetables, flowers, minor forest produce and their value-added products

b. Duty-free import of capital goods under EPCG scheme

c. Development of agro-export zones

d. Import of seeds, bulbs, tubers and planting material liberalised

e. Export of liberalised plant portions, derivatives and extracts to promote export of medicinal plants and herbal products

The three Exim policies launched since 1992 were distinct. The first policy (1992) aimed at import and export Liberalization. The second policy (1997) oriented towards globalization. The third policy (2004) recognised, for the first time, the importance of trade as an instrument of growth. All policies related to agro-food are based on the premise that India has vast potential for export and emphasise the need to harness this potential. To actualise this, various restrictions and controls on export of various agricultural items have been gradually removed, institutional and infrastructural support has been strengthened and some indirect incentives have been put in place. However, agro-food imports continued to be considered undesirable. QRs on imports of agricultural products were phased out by April 2001 after WTO ruled that QRs were not justified on balance-of-payment grounds and recommended that India's import regime should conform to its WTO obligations. The only agricultural item for which real Liberalization of import has taken place is vegetable oil. Its import could not be checked by even very high level of import duty. Import of other agricultural items is encouraged when domestic supply cannot match domestic demand, e.g. pulses, and in case of temporary supply shocks, such as in the case of cotton and sugar and earlier even in the case of wheat.

There have been significant departures from the stated policy depending on developments in global and domestic economies. For instance, emphasis on export Liberalization and import duty underwent significant changes after 2006–07, when global prices started increasing with the onset of the global food crisis. Following the crisis, India almost reversed some aspects of trade policy to insulate its domestic market from global food prices. It banned the export of main staples – rice and wheat (Table 1). The ban was relaxed after four years in 2011. During this period (2007–11), agricultural trade was strictly regulated by various notifications issued by the Directorate General of Foreign Trade. There was also a steep reduction in import duty on vegetable oils, which constituted more than one third of India's agro-food import. Customs duty on refined vegetable oil has been brought down to 7.5 per cent and import of crude vegetable oil is free of any duty (Table 3).

C. Trade Flows

During early 1980s, India met a part of its agro-food demand from imports, and imports constituted close to 4 per cent of India's agriculture output. Further, agricultural (crop and livestock sector) import exceeded agricultural export marginally. This sector did not generate any trade surplus during early 1980s. During late 1980s, attaining and improving self-sufficiency in food – particularly in edible oil, which formed the bulk of agricultural imports – was strongly emphasised. As a result, agricultural imports declined to less than one third and the ratio of import to domestic production dropped to less than 1 per cent between 1981–82 and 1990–91. In contrast, exports witnessed an increase, though quite small. Agricultural exports witnessed an exponential growth in the later 1990s though there was a decrease in between for a short period (Fig. 1). Between 1991–92 and 2008–09, India's agro-exports increased from $2.8 billion to $15.6 billion, and agricultural imports increased ten times, from $0.67 billion to $6.77 billion. Exports exceeded imports by more than $ 2 billion during early 1990s, thus generating a surplus. The trade surplus almost doubled by 1996–97 followed by a large squeeze during late 1990s, which wiped out the increase witnessed during initial years of reforms. Agriculture trade surplus surged after 2003–04. Exports exceeded imports by $10.7 billion during 2007–08 recording the highest level of trade surplus generated by the agriculture sector in the country.

Ratio measures such as export, import and net trade divided by total domestic production are better indicator than absolute figures for capturing openness, trade performance and integration of the domestic economy with the global economy. Complete information on these indicators from 1990–91 to 2009–10 is depicted in Fig. 2. The ratio of trade (export and import) to domestic production[24] has followed a steady

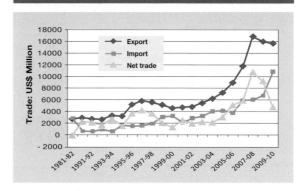

Figure 1   Trade in agriculture food products 1981-82 to 2009-10

Source: 1. Indian Agriculture in Brief, 21st edition, Ministry of Agriculture, GOI, New Delhi
2. Agricultural Statistics at a Glance, Ministry of Agriculture, GOI, New Delhi.

increase after 1990–91, which indicates rising openness and increase in the integration of the domestic economy with the global economy. Exports constituted less than 3 per cent and imports constituted less than 1 per cent of total agricultural (crop and livestock sector) output in early 1990s. These ratios went past 7 and 3 per cent, respectively, in the next two decades. However, this change has not been smooth and is characterised by various phases. Interestingly, these phases coincided with the movement in global food prices. As the index of global food prices increased from 118 during early 1990s to 149 during 1996–97, the proportion of exports in value of agricultural output increased from around 3 per cent to more than 5 per cent. After 1996–97, as global food prices declined, the proportion of agriculture production sold overseas also followed a decline. Once again, when global prices started rising after 2001–02, the ratio of export to output followed suit. Between 2003–04 and 2008–09, global food prices increased by 83 per cent and the ratio of export to output increased by 62 per cent. The close and strong association between export orientation of Indian agriculture and global food prices is clearly visible in Figs. 2 and 3. Post-1990–91 period can be clearly divided in three phases: phase of modest increase in global food prices (1990–91 to 1996–97), phase of decline in global food prices (1997–98 to 2002–03) and phase of rapid increase in global food prices (2003–04 to 2008–09). The share of India's agriculture export in total domestic production also presents a similar pattern. The correlation between global food prices and the proportion of domestic production sold outside the country was 0.85 during last two decades.

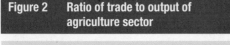

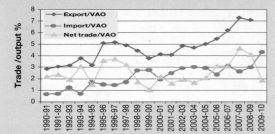

Figure 2   Ratio of trade to output of agriculture sector

Source: 1. Agricultural Statistics at a Glance,
Ministry of Agriculture, GOI, New Delhi.
2. National Accounts Statistics,
Central Statistical Organization, New Delhi.

Figure 3   Global Food Price Index base 2000=100

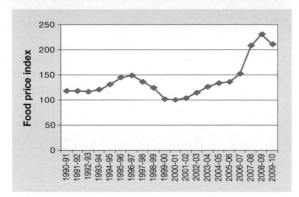

Source: Commodity Price Data, Pink Sheet, World Bank.

Unlike export, the ratio of import to domestic production has shown more or less a rising trend since 1990–91 irrespective of changes in global food prices (Fig. 2). Imports constituted less than 1 per cent of value of agriculture output during early 1990s. In the next decade, the ratio of import to domestic output more than doubled. There was a further increase in import intensity of agriculture during the next 10 years. The association between import share in domestic production and global prices was found statistically non-significant up to 5 per cent level with the correlation coefficient being 0.35 (Table 4).

Table 4   Linear correlation between trade ratios and global food price index

Trade ratio	Correlation	Level of significance
Export to output	0.85	0.99
Import to output	0.35	Not significant up to 0.95
Net trade to output	0.84	0.99

To sum up, the surplus generated through agriculture trade (export – imports) has seen tremendous increase since 1990–91. Agriculture exports exceeded imports by $2 billion during early 1990s. The trade surplus increased to $4 billion during 1996–97. There was a dip in the net trade for some time from 1998–99 to 2004–05 owing to stagnation in exports. When agriculture export picked up with strengthening of global food prices, net trade also witnessed a very sharp increase in absolute value as well as in relation to the growth of domestic agricultural output. Thus, like exports, the ratio of net trade to domestic output closely followed the movement in international food prices. The correlation between the two was 0.84, which is highly significant. It emerges that the opening up of the economy since 1991 has been much more favourable for agricultural export than for agricultural imports. Export performance of Indian agriculture is critically dependent on the global price situation. Hence, we can infer that India's agricultural exports do not have strong competitive edge as exports shrink considerably when the global price situation turns unfavourable.

D. Changes in composition of trade

The opening up of trade by India affected the export and import of various commodities in different ways. Accordingly, the composition of agricultural exports and imports has undergone a significant change since 1991. These changes are shown in Table 5 for exports and Table 6 for imports. Interestingly, some commodities appear in both export and import commodities. Since early 1990s, agricultural exports grew at annual compound growth rate close to 12 per cent and imports have increased at the rate of 15.3 per cent. Tea and coffee, which were important traditional export items from India, showed less than 4 per cent growth, which comprised almost one third of the growth in total agricultural export. As a result, their share in agricultural export fell from 20.7 per cent during 1991–92 to 1994–95 to 7.0 per cent during 2006–07 to 2009–10.

Much hyped horticulture exports grew at a lower rate than that of total farm exports. Further, horticulture imports have risen at a higher rate than exports. Cotton and jute export showed the highest growth among all major groups, closely followed by livestock products. India has also increased its sugar export by more than 10 times during the last two decades, though these exports are highly fluctuating. India is known for importing huge quantity of vegetable oil.[25] Important initiatives were launched during late 1980s to reduce dependence on imported edible oil and attain self-sufficiency. These efforts were helpful in raising oilseed output and domestic production of vegetable oils. However, this did not reduce dependence on imports as domestic consumption rose rapidly. Since early 1990s, the import of edible oil has increased from less than half a million tonne to close to 8 million tonne. In value terms, vegetable oil import increased from $106 million to $3.5 billion in recent years, thus registering an annual increase of 26 per cent. Also worth noting is that edible oil import accounted for more than 47 per cent of total agricultural imports in recent years compared with 12 per cent during early 1990s.

It is interesting to point out that though India's oilseeds sector is repeatedly criticised for very high import dependence, the impressive performance of oilseed sector in export has escaped attention. Oil meal and oilseed export from India has experienced annual growth close to 10 per cent since early 1990s. This has led to an annual export of these products to $3 billion during 2006–07 to 2009–10. Thus, close to 90 per cent of import bill of vegetable oil is met by oilseed export.[26] The share of food grains in exports and imports has increased. India has remained a net exporter of rice for a long time. However, it has remained at the mar-

gin of self-sufficiency in the case of wheat –exporting and importing depending on fluctuations in domestic production. Pulses have emerged as an important import item in food grains. The share of food grains has shown a significant increase in total export and a sharp decline in import. Food grains now (2006–07 to 2009–10) constitute one fourth of agricultural imports and one fifth of agricultural exports, with a trade surplus of more than $1 billion.

In the post-WTO period, India's plantation sector has faced a stiff global competition. Despite this, spice export recorded an annual growth of 13.6 per cent. Although spice import increased at a much higher rate than exports, the annual earnings from exports during the four years ending 2009–10 were more than four times the value of imports.

E. Integration between Domestic and International Prices

As mentioned earlier, till early 1990s, domestic prices of most agricultural commodities in India were insulated from the world market by various instruments such as trade ban, QRs, canalization, and licenses. Overvalued exchange rate further acted as a check on deriving any advantage that may result from ex-

Table 5   Changes in composition of agricultural exports from 1991–92 to 2009–10

	Export: $ million		Trend growth rate	Composition: %		
	1991–92 to 1994–95	2006–07 to 2009–10		1991–92 to 1994–95	2006–07 to 2009–10	Change in share
Cereals	384	2940	14.54	16.4	25.8	9.33
Pulses	18	129	14.18	0.8	1.1	0.38
Tea and coffee	564	1006	3.93	20.7	7.0	-13.74
Spices	166	1123	13.59	6.1	7.8	1.72
Horticulture	507	1942	9.36	18.7	13.5	-5.13
Livestock	109	1318	18.06	4.0	9.2	5.17
Oilseed and oil meal	740	3032	9.85	27.2	21.1	-6.11
Sugar and molasses	66	798	18.11	2.4	5.6	3.14
Cotton and jute	110	1659	19.82	4.1	11.6	7.51
Miscellaneous	54	402	14.31	2.0	2.8	0.81
Tobacco	136	615	10.55	5.0	4.3	-0.74
Total agriculture	2718	14349	11.73	100.0	100.0	—

Source: Agricultural Statistics at a Glance, Ministry of Agriculture, GOI, New Delhi.

Table 6	Changes in composition of agricultural imports: 1991–92 to 2009–10						
	Import: million $		Trend growth rate	Composition: Per cent			
	1991–92 to 1994–95	2006–07 to 2009–10		1991–92 to 1994–95	2006–07 to 2009–10	Change in share	
Cereals	131.6	569.0	10.3	15.1	7.7	-7.4	
Pulses	147.4	1412.3	16.3	16.9	19.0	2.2	
Tea and coffee	0.0	40.8	0.0	0.0	0.6	0.6	
Spices	10.4	237.3	23.2	1.2	3.2	2.0	
Horticulture	222.1	1028.4	10.8	25.4	13.9	-11.5	
Livestock	6.5	9.7	2.7	0.7	0.1	-0.6	
Vegetable oil	106.1	3493.2	26.2	12.1	47.1	35.0	
Sugar and molasses	182.0	345.8	4.4	20.8	4.7	-16.2	
Cotton and jute	68.0	280.8	9.9	7.8	3.8	-4.0	
Total agriculture	874.2	7417.3	15.3	100.0	100.0	--	
Tobacco	136	615	10.55	5.0	4.3	-0.74	
Total agriculture	2718	14349	11.73	100.0	100.0	—	

Source: Agricultural Statistics at a Glance, Ministry of Agriculture, GOI, New Delhi.

ports. However, with the Liberalization of agricultural trade which started gradually in 1991 and intensified after the implementation of WTO agreement in 1995, agricultural trade has witnessed tremendous increase. The ratio of trade to domestic production was below 5 per cent till 1994–95 and started increasing steadily thereafter. During 2008–09, India's agriculture trade with other countries reached 11 per cent of value of agricultural output and 13.6 per cent of GDP agriculture. The increase in the ratio of trade to output after 1994–95 has been associated with a significant increase in integration of domestic and global prices. Table 7 shows the simple correlation between domes-

tic and international prices, expressed in dollars. The correlation was below 0.3 in the case of maize, rice, wheat and sugar during 1981–95. It increased to more than 0.8 for rice, wheat and sugar for 1996–2009.

F. Free Trade versus Strategic Opening Up

Despite significant Liberalization, trade in agriculture continues to be regulated as India has preferred strategic opening up rather than complete free trade. The country adjusts its trade policy depending on domestic production and price situation and global situation. *The guiding principle for the opening up has been to allow domestic prices to move in tandem with the trend in global prices but insulate against sharp spike and troughs.* Table 8 shows this. The table presents two scenarios of global prices. Years 2001 and 2009 represent low-price and high-price scenarios, respectively. Global food price index with base 2000=100 was 103 in 2001 and 205 in 2009 (Commodity Price Data, Pink Sheet, World Bank, 2011).

During 2001, when global prices were low, India did not put any restrictions on the export of most agricultural commodities but imposed a very high duty on import to prevent cheap imports from depressing do-

Table 7	Correlation between domestic and world prices of selected commodities			
Period	Maize	Rice	Wheat	Sugar
1981–1995	0.122	0.165	0.198	0.286
1996–2009	0.753	0.808	0.835	0.877

Note: Domestic prices are for Delhi market for wheat and rice, Bengaluru for maize, and Muzzafarnagar, UP, for sugar. International prices refer to maize US no. 2 fob Gulf, rice Thai 5 per cent broken, wheat US HRW 1, sugar world.
Source: 1. Commodity Price Data, Pink sheet, World Bank.
2. Agricultural Prices in India, Directorate of Economics and Statistics, MOA, GOI, New Delhi.

Table 8	Trade and price policy during different phases of global prices				
Policy instrument	Year	Wheat	Rice	Groundnut oil	Sugar
International price	2001	127	173		190
	2009	224	555		400
Import duty	2001	50	80	75–85	60
	2009	0	70	0	0
Export	2001	Free	Free	Free	Free
	2009	Banned	Non-basmati: ban Basmati: MEP	Banned or Restricted	Banned
Increase in MSP	2001	5.2	4.1	5.6	6.1
	2009	17.6	11.1	35.5	59.9

Source: Commodity Price data, Pink Sheet, World Bank; Agricultural Statistics at a Glance, Ministry of Agriculture, GOI, New Delhi.
Abbreviations: MEP, minimum export price; MSP, minimum support price.

mestic prices (Table 8). Thus, during the period of low global prices, India followed a trade policy that protected producers' interest. Similarly, when international prices were low, minimum support price (MSP) was raised by a small amount. Global food and agricultural prices started showing steep increase after 2006, and the period 2007–09 witnessed a spike in food prices. During the global food crisis, India reversed its policy from what it was during low global prices (2000–01). Imports were freely allowed but exports were banned or restricted. The logic behind this was to prevent a steep hike in domestic prices due to the transmission of global price effect. Therefore, the trade policy was used to protect consumers against abnormal increase in global prices. MSP, on the other hand, was given a steep hike during these years in order to minimise the gap between global prices and domestic prices. MSPs for wheat and rice were raised by 17.6 and 11.1 per cent, respectively, during 2009 and groundnut prices were raised by 36 per cent in the same year. These increases were much higher than the rise in MSP during the phase of low global prices, when they were raised by less than 6 per cent.

Further, during 2009, the Directorate General of Foreign Trade, New Delhi, issued 17 notifications relating to export and import of agro-food products to effectively regulate and control trade flows. This explains the entire logic underlying the changes in India's trade policy after the opening up of economy.

G. Trade Openness and Regional Equity

After the opening up of economy, trade flows and trade pattern followed significant changes. Two major changes in agriculture trade have had an impact on a large part of population: (a) increase in net export of cereals, primarily rice, and (b) increase in import of vegetable oils. As a result, domestic prices of cereals and oilseeds have moved closer to global prices. This implies that cereal prices in the domestic market have moved up and oilseed prices have come down. As India is a vast and diverse country, with different regions following different cropping pattern, changes in trade pattern have affected different regions differently. The states and regions with net surplus in cereals may benefit from the opening up, which involves rise in cereal prices. The states and regions with a net deficit in cereals may be adversely affected. The reverse holds true in case of the opening up of edible oil imports. Further, states also differ in terms of economic development, per capita income and consumption pattern. Rice is the staple food in some states while wheat is the prominent food in others. Depending on climatic conditions, states specialise in the production of different crops. Therefore, trade Liberalization will affect different states in different ways. No serious attempt has been made to estimate the effect of trade Liberalization on different states of India at the sectoral or economy level. One study (Chand 1999b) looked at the state-wise impact of trade Liberalization, focussing on rice and wheat. It revealed that Punjab was the main beneficiary of trade Liberalization in rice and wheat, followed by Haryana, while small positive gains accrued to Uttar Pradesh, West Bengal and Madhya Pradesh. The remaining states, which constituted about 63 per cent population of the country, were losers from grain trade Liberalization. Among the 12 loser states, 10 had per capita income lower than the national average. The overall relationship between the per capita income of a state and net social gain was positive and significant. This implied that higher the per capita income of a state, more the gain from Liberalization of trade in wheat and rice, and lower the per capita income of a state, higher the loss due to the Liberalization.

H. Trade versus Stock for Price Stabilization

Buffer stocks have been used by the government as an important instrument of price stabilization. However, this involved a heavy cost in terms of procurement, handling, carrying, storage, etc. This has increasingly become fiscally unsustainable. As an alternative, it has been suggested that the government should use varying tariffs on external trade to stabilise domestic prices; when international prices are low, tariff on import should be kept high to provide price support to domestic producers, and when international prices increase, tariffs should be reduced. Similarly, variable levies on export can be worked out for net exporting countries (Jha and Srinivasan, 1999). Jha and Srinivasan found the trade option to be superior to buffer stock in stabilising prices under liberalised trade regime. Their findings were refuted by Chand (2003), who contended that owing to high volatility in global prices, any comparison of trade option with stock option could result in a different conclusion depending on the magnitude of international price in that particular year. Thus, to find out whether trade option is more economical than buffer stock for domestic price stabilization, one needs to consider a longer period, as it will cover various phases of price movements. To accomplish this, Chand (2003) compared export parity price during a year of above-normal production and import parity price during a year of below-normal production with economic cost of grain to the Food Corporation of India (FCI) by selecting a long period of 26 years (1975 to 2000). The study assumed that interyear price stability requires government purchase exceeding the trend output and sale from buffer stock to the tune of deficiency of output from the trend output.

The comparison of trade option with the policy of buffer stock for the domestic stabilization of wheat price shows that out of the 16 years during which domestic supply fell short of the trend, in 10 years the cost of meeting the supply deficit from domestic sources (economic cost to FCI) was lower than the import parity price (Table 9). In 6 years, meeting the shortfall in supply by imports was cheaper for maintaining stability in domestic supply. If domestic wholesale price is assumed to be the outcome of government policy of price stabilization, then its comparison with the net price that can be earned from sale of produce in the international market during the years of above-normal production indicates gain/loss to producers from domestic price stabilization. Wheat production was above normal in 11 out of 26 years. Out of these 11 years, the price realised from export was lower in 10 years. Selling in the international market would have fetched better price than that available under government intervention in only three of these years.

A comparison of domestic stabilization measures for rice shows that during the 12 years since 1975, when output was short of the trend, import was more cost-effective option than domestic stabilization in only 2 out of 12 years. In the second scenario, when the actual output exceeded the trend, domestic producers could earn better from export in only 5 out of 14 years. In the remaining 9 years, the government-determined domestic wholesale price was higher than export parity price. This analysis shows that among the two options – stabilization through buffer stock and trade – the latter was costlier than the former mostly though this also depends on fluctuation in international prices. Because of this experience, even after Liberalization of trade, buffer stock continues to be an important instrument of price stabilization in India.

Table 9	Frequency distribution of superiority of trade v/s buffer stock as stabilization measures (1974–2000)				
Particular	**Production scene: Wheat**		**Production scene: Rice**	
	Above normal	Below normal	Above normal	Below normal
	Frequency		Frequency	
Target of stabilization →	Producers	Consumers	Producers	Consumers
Trade better option than buffer stock	1	5	2	5
Buffer stock better option than trade	10	11	10	9

Source: Chand (2003).

I. Opening Up and Crisis Management

The changes taking place in the global economy and various factors related to climate change and global warming are causing severe, and often abrupt, fluctuations in global food and agricultural prices. These fluctuations turned abnormally high during 2007–08 and created a sort of global food crisis. It is feared that supply shocks for agro-food commodities are likely to become more severe and more frequent and will persist for longer periods. These changes are likely to exacerbate the already high volatility in international food prices. The experience of 2007 and 2008, when the world faced the food crisis following abnormal increase in global food prices, shows that India has effectively protected its market and managed its food situation comfortably. However, some countries were badly hit. Year on year inflation in India in any month during 2007–08 in wheat and rice remained below 11 per cent, whereas global prices showed more than 100 per cent inflation in wheat and more than 200 per cent annual rate of inflation in rice during early months of 2008 (Figs. 4 and 5). Similarly, food price inflation in India did not exceed 11 per cent, whereas global food inflation exceeded 40 per cent in early months of 2008. It is quite useful to explore how India could escape the wrath of food crisis on its domestic food prices.

Figure 5	Annual rate of inflation in rice prices (percentage)

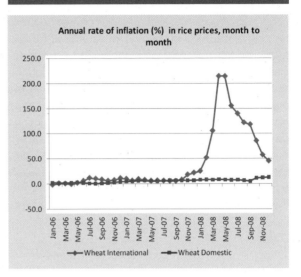

Figure 4	Annual rate of inflation in wheat prices (percentage)

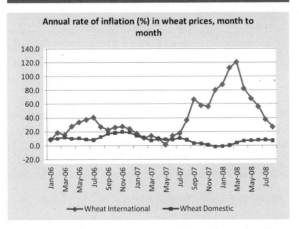

After the Liberalization of external trade, India liberalised its domestic market by revoking many provisions of the Essential Commodities Act (1955). The Central Government issued the "Removal of Licensing requirements, Stock limits and Movement Restrictions on Specified Foodstuffs Order, 2002" on 15 February 2002. This allowed dealers to freely buy, stock, sell, transport, distribute, dispose, etc., any quantity of wheat, paddy/rice, coarse grains, sugar, edible oilseeds and edible oils without requiring any government license or permit. This was followed by launching of futures trading in wheat and rice in 2003. In another important step, the Central Government and various state governments adopted the Model Agriculture Produce Market Committee (APMC) Act, which facilitated direct contract between buyers (trading firm/processor, exporter) and producers/farmers for the purchase of produce, commonly known as contract farming.

Private trade responded very quickly to take advantage of this situation. Futures trading in wheat started moving in tandem with CBOT future prices. This raised domestic prices of staple food and they attained equilibrium with global prices. Wheat prices in India during some months in 2005–06 and 2006–07 increased by almost the same per cent as the price increase in the global market (US HRW). While wheat prices during 2005–06 remained under strong upward pressure, wheat harvest during 2005–06 (refers to wheat harvested during March–May 2006) turned out to be lower than normal and lower than anticipated. On account of strong pressure on wheat prices and poor harvest during 2006, public agencies could procure only 9.226 million tonne of wheat against the target of 15 million tonne. By paying a little more than MSP, the private sector succeeded in attracting farmers to sell wheat to it. Thus, the wheat stock available with the government on 1 July 2006 was only 8.2 million tonne against a minimum norm of 17.1 million tonne, and food grain stock was 19.3 million tonne as against norm of 26.9 million tonne. This decline in stocks and the strain on food grain supply coincided with a similar supply situation at the global level. Following a rising trend in global food prices and low stock with public agencies, the Indian Government took four major decisions.[27] First, it started importing wheat through the State Trading Corporation at a price higher than the one prevailing in the country. Second, futures trading in wheat and rice was banned. Third, some restrictions on the private sector were brought back. Government decision to import had a strong effect on open-market food prices (Chand, 2007). Fourth, wheat and rice export was restricted or banned. This experience reveals that following factors helped India safeguard against the adverse impact of the global food crisis (Chand, 2009):

1. Active government participation in rice and wheat market
2. Institutional mechanism for dealing with price instability
3. Intelligent monitoring of domestic and global prices and supply situation
4. Prompt policy action to maintain price stability
5. Frequent changes in regulation to curve private sector's profiteering activities
6. Changes in trade policy in response to global changes
7. Social safety network

Therefore, Chand (2009) concluded that market forces cannot provide safeguard against global shocks. Hence, government intervention is essential to safeguard domestic economies and vulnerable population from global shocks and volatility. It is asserted that this cannot be done without appropriate institutional mechanisms. These mechanisms cannot be created to respond to just a crisis situation; rather they need to be in place permanently.

J. Balancing Producers and Consumers Interest

Table 10 presents some important characteristics of India's agricultural producers and consumers. Agricultural producers – 47 per cent of total households – form a large segment of Indian society. Agriculture is the main occupation for more than 50 per cent of the country's total workforce. Thus, the state of agriculture is crucial for the livelihood of majority of the country's population. Further, more than 83 per cent farm holdings are less than 2 hectare in size. The av-

erage holding size in the country is 1.3 hectare. The average producer in the country is weak in terms of resources and income and not in a position to bear economic shocks. A recent study found that farm income of 62 per cent farmers in India was lower than that needed to remain above poverty line. Such farmers are highly vulnerable to (downward) price fluctuations. Most of the farmers in India can't quickly and easily switch from one crop to another to adjust to sharp fluctuations in market prices. Thus, maintaining a stable and remunerative price environment for producers is accorded high priority in the domestic policy and also in the trade policy. Consumers – the other segment of the society– are a highly heterogeneous group with wide variation in income. However, like the average producer, average consumer in the country is in a weak economic position. About 37 per cent of the population is below poverty line (according to the report of Tendulkar Committee, set up by the Planning Commission). Poverty ratio is 41.6 per cent according to per capita daily income of $1.25. The average rural consumer spends 57 per cent and the average urban consumer spends 43 per cent of total household expenditure on food. Thus, an increase in food prices by, say 10 per cent, implies a rural consumer spends 5.7 per cent more and urban consumer spends 4.3 per cent more to maintain the same level of food consumption. Thus, any significant increase in price without corresponding increase in income will affect both the incidence of poverty and nutrition.

A vast majority of producers and consumers in the country is vulnerable and not in a position to absorb price shocks. In this situation, policymakers face a delicate task of balancing producers' and consumers' interests. Transmission of high global prices, which is favourable for producers and adverse for consumers, is moderated through checks

Table 10	Some important characteristics of producers and consumers in India	
Average size of land holding; hectare		1.30
Small and marginal farmers (%) below 2.0 hectare		83.0
Workforce in agriculture as (%) of total workforce		53.0
Share of food in total household expenditure (%): Rural Urban		57 44
Population below poverty (2004–05) based on 1$/day income		41.6

on export. Conversely, transmission of low international prices, which is favourable for consumers and adverse for producers, is moderated through varying tariffs appropriately and checking imports. Import duty is kept low when international prices are high or domestic prices are high, and import duty is raised when prices are low. Besides trade policy measures, domestic prices are also influenced by the system of minimum support price implemented through public procurement and through open-market sales by the FCI, by liquidating the stocks held by it. The underlying logic is to protect consumers against high prices and to safeguard producers' interest against low prices. Past experience shows that there are times when producers can get higher prices if exports are freely allowed. There are also times when domestic prices are higher than international prices and also higher than the cif price. In the first situation, producers are prevented from getting a higher price through export restrictions, and in the second situation, consumers cannot source a product at a lower price on account of import restrictions. From the policy angle, in the first situation consumers' interest is protected and in the second situation producers' interest is protected. As international prices swing upward and downward, trade policy sometimes secures producers' interest and at other times consumers' interest.

K. Conclusions

The Liberalization of agriculture trade in India has led to a sharp increase in volumes of imports and exports. This has resulted in substantial increase in surplus from agriculture trade. The ratio of trade to domestic production of agricultural commodity moves in tandem with the movement in global food prices. Exports have shown considerable sensitivity to global food prices; imports, on the contrary, have been increasing steadily irrespective of changes in global food prices. Hence, one can infer that India's agriculture exports lack strong competitive edge.

The composition of trade has also seen large variations after Liberalization. Exports have been rising at the rate of 12 per cent and imports at the rate of 15.3 per cent. However, this was not driven by growth in traditional items of trade such as tea and coffee or horticulture but by product groups such as livestock products, sugar, cotton and jute, and cereals for exports and vegetable oils, spices and pulses for imports. Food grains have increased their share in both

exports and imports. India continues to remain a net exporter of rice and at the margin of self-sufficiency in wheat. The value of India's agriculture trade is now 13.6 per cent of agriculture GDP and 11 per cent of the value of agriculture output. The integration of domestic and global prices is held responsible for the increase in ratio of agriculture trade to output. The correlation between domestic and international prices of maize, rice, wheat and sugar rose substantially during 1976–2000.The Indian Government is faced with a key question: Should it follow free trade policy in agriculture or adopt strategic opening up? The path followed till now has been to open economy and allow domestic prices to move in line with the trend in the global prices but insulate it against sharp crests and troughs. Following the Liberalization of trade, domestic prices of cereals and oilseeds have come closer to global prices. Thus, an increase in cereal prices and decrease in oilseed prices benefit the states that have a surplus in cereals and hurt those which face deficit in cereals and surplus in oilseeds. As states differ in their level of economic development, their per capita income and consumption patterns, the resulting effects of Liberalization on them differs. The trade pattern that has emerged after Liberalization has been favourable for states with higher per capita income and adverse for the states with lower per capita income. This raises an important equity issue for a large country with diverse agriculture.

The supply and price shocks in both global as well as domestic prices are becoming more frequent, more severe and much longer. Thus, price stabilization assumes greater importance. A comparison of buffer stock versus trade (import/export) for domestic market stabilization following fluctuations in domestic production shows that in an overwhelming number of cases buffer stock is a better option than trade to protect consumer and producer interest. Similarly, prompt changes in trade policy, buffer stock and domestic regulation have helped India safeguard against transmission of effects of global food crisis during 2007–08. This policy has been effective in balancing producers' and consumers' interests. Strong evidence suggests that strategic Liberalization rather than free trade in agriculture should continue to be the cornerstone of India's opening up of agro-food sector to the world economy. India's experience with trade Liberalization offers some important lessons, which are as follows:

- Regulated trade instead of free trade provides effective safeguards against transmission

- of adverse effects of price swings on producers and consumers.
- Appropriate variation in tariffs provides a useful instrument for regulating trade and protection against short-term price fluctuations.
- Allowing domestic prices to move along the trend in international prices helps in reaping benefit of trade, but the trend and volatility in prices need to be clearly differentiated.
- Aligning domestic prices with changes in international prices regularly and dovetailing domestic policy with trade policy are quite effective in balancing producer and consumer interest.
- Increase in frequency and intensity of global price and supply shocks requires intelligent monitoring of domestic and global prices and supply situation.

This necessitates prompt policy action to maintain price stability.
- Dealing with various types of trade shocks requires well-established mechanisms; such mechanisms cannot be created at the time of shocks.
- Domestic public sector capacity for market intervention through stocks is quite significant in protecting producers during low domestic prices and consumers during high prices. Trade alone cannot be very effective in maintaining domestic price stability.
- Strategic Liberalization, based on international price situation, rather than free trade, is very effective in guarding against international shocks and crises.
- Trade policy can be a very useful instrument in balancing producer and consumer interest over a period of time.

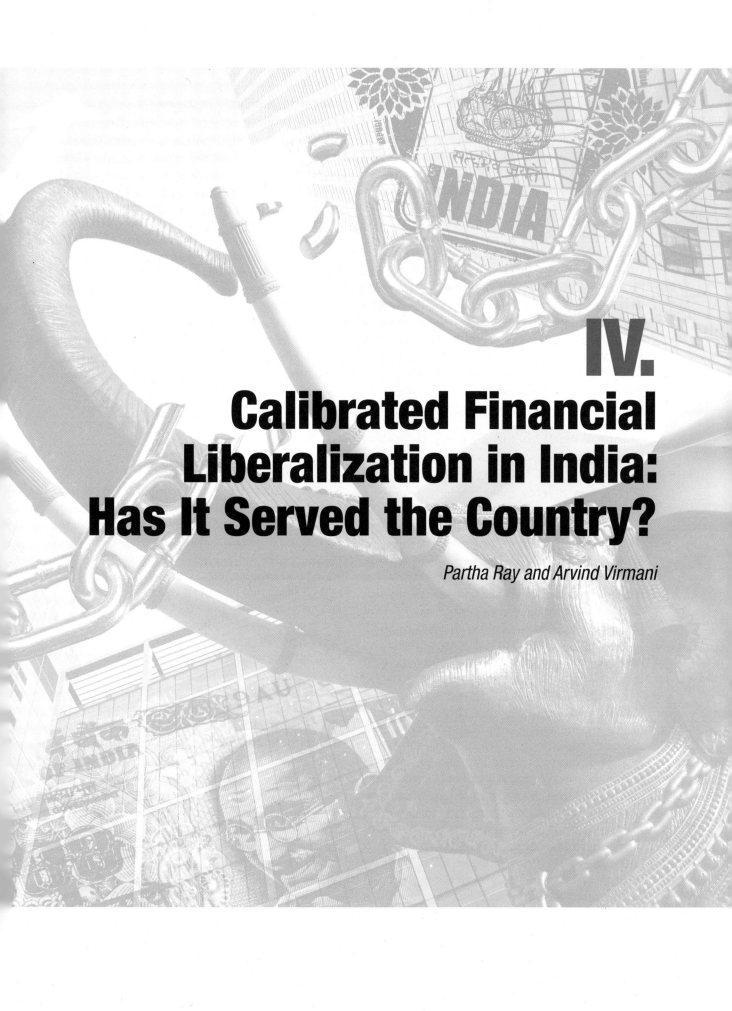

IV.
Calibrated Financial Liberalization in India: Has It Served the Country?

Partha Ray and Arvind Virmani

A. Introduction

The policymaker devising a financial Liberalization program is often faced with a choice of cold-turkey approach versus the gradualism approach. While it is not a zero-one choice, economy-specific discussions of economic Liberalization in general and financial Liberalization in particular start with a priori. Depending on the ideological location of the exponent, the pace of Liberalization is frequently labelled "fast" and "slow". This chapter argues that such branding of the pace of Liberalization suffers from an inherent over-simplification and that economy-specific contexts need to be appreciated before pronouncing any value judgement about the pace of reform. At the risk of repeating a cliché, the analogy could be one of driving a car where depending on the road condition, the driver needs to zero in on an optimal application of the gas paddle vis-à-vis brakes. To say that driving was slow or fast without any reference to the road condition is intrinsically misleading. Without trivialising the analogy, this chapter presents an analytical account of the financial Liberalization in India.[28]

To begin with, it may be useful to set the context and refer to a working definition of "financial Liberalization". In the paradigm of "financial repression", the repressed domestic financial sectors are characterised by widespread bankruptcies, massive government interventions or nationalizations of private institutions, and low domestic savings and financial Liberalization generally sought to free domestic capital markets from government-induced distortions (McKinnon 1973; Shaw, 1973). Four features of financial repression have been emphasised: (a) explicit or indirect capping or control over interest rates; (b) government ownership or control of domestic banks and financial institutions (FIs) and barriers to entry of other institutions into the market; (c) creation or maintenance of a captive domestic market for government debt achieved by requiring domestic banks to hold government debt; and (d) government restrictions on the transfer of assets abroad through capital controls (Reinhart and Sbrancia, 2011). Historically, many countries tended to have restricted competition in the financial sector with plethora of modes of government interventions and regulations – Financial Liberalization from this viewpoint was referred to as winding of a regulation that inhibited the free play of markets forces in financial markets.[29] While "equity" was cited as the logic behind such restrictions, the government's intention to capture a large piece of the finance pie (particularly in

absence of fiscal prudence) cannot be ruled out.

There were a number of critiques of the "financial repression" paradigm. Within the mainstream thinking, the emergence of information-asymmetry (where borrowers have different probability of repayment but banks cannot identify "good" borrowers from "bad", and prices act as a screening device) showed that in a competitive equilibrium a loan market may be characterised by "credit rationing" and the interest rate a bank charges may itself affect the riskiness of a pool of loans either by sorting potential borrowers (adverse selection) or by affecting borrowers' actions (moral hazard) (Stiglitz and Weiss, 1981; Virmani, 1982). Subsequently, the literature on banks as "delegated monitors" established, in some sense, a role for a visible hand of regulation in the financial sector (Diamond and Dybvig, 1983). Illustratively, it has been shown that in a fully liberalised and competitive banking economy, banks may fail to finance potential industrial entrepreneurs because of poaching externality and may systematically favour short-term projects with front-loaded returns at the expense of projects with strong learning effects (Emran and Stiglitz, 2008). Empirically as well, it has been shown that intrinsic imperfections of any financial market posed dilemmas to a policymaker and that any "pell-mell deregulation of commercial banks" could have unintended consequences (Diaz Alazandro, 1985). There was parallel literature on the relationship between finance and growth which states that countries with better functioning banks and markets grow faster (irrespective of the degree to which a country is bank-based or market-based) and that better functioning financial systems ease external financing constraints that impede firm and industrial expansion (Levine, 2005). Regarding international policy, various efforts by the Bank of International Settlement showed that financial Liberalization is often accompanied by a parallel process of prudential regulation. The clamour of financial reregulation has come up as an aftermath of the global financial crisis, and various efforts by the Financial Stability Board/G-20 and various standard-setting bodies bear testimony to this.

While it would be impossible and unwarranted to summarise the rather large literature on financial Liberalization in the present chapter, it needs to be appreciated that in popular parlance, discussion of issues related to "financial Liberalization" often gets caricatured as a "state *versus* market" debate. Nothing could be further from truth. In fact, corner positions or binary conclusions are not representative depiction of empirical reality of financial sector Liberalization. The experience is perhaps much more complicated. The complications often stem because the frequent empirical measurement of "financial development/Liberalization" does not capture the concepts emerging from theoretical models very accurately. How best to measure financial Liberalization? Increasing availability of quantum of finance, downward and freer movement of interest rates, institutional development in the realm of finance – a researcher is fraught with multiple options. Furthermore, at a level of abstraction, one can distinguish between various dimensions of financial Liberalization – Liberalization of FIs vis-à-vis financial markets, Liberalization of domestic banking sector (and of related financial intermediaries) vis-à-vis current and capital account in the external payments front. In this chapter, our endeavour will be rather eclectic and our aim will be to give a flavour of various aspects of financial Liberalization in a country like India.

Financial Liberalization was an integral part of the Indian reforms strategy. Thus, to view it in isolation will be inappropriate. In fact, the Indian experience of financial Liberalization has attempted to lessen the extent of financial repression in all the four spheres that we have emphasised earlier. However, its pace was calibrated – It differed across sectors and markets. Consequently, there are conflicting views regarding whether its pace was somewhat slow or roughly right given the subjective and objective condition of the economy. While the corner views do not converge, we believe the issue of pace is not a binary choice. In fact, one needs to be much more nuanced in pronouncing any judgement on the efficacy of financial sector reform in India, particularly in view of the favourable outcome as well as absence of the counterfactual in many cases. The rest

of the chapter is organised fairly simplistically. To set the context, Section 2 traces the development of the Indian financial sector till 1991. Section 3 is devoted to financial Liberalization in domestic and external payments in India since 1991. Section 4 concludes the chapter.

B. The Pre-1990's Financial Scenario: Achievements and Pitfalls

1.   Financial Intermediaries

As a prelude to India's financial Liberalization, it is useful to have a quick rundown of India's financial sector policies and situation during the 1970s and 1980s. While the Indian banking sector in early 1950s was reasonably free, there were a number of instances of bank failures during the 1950s and 1960s, and accordingly, bank consolidation took place during the 1960s. As banking considered a means of both resource mobilization and allocation of scarce credit in "desirable" sectors of economic activity, it was essentially seen as an arm of the Five Pear Planning mechanism. Towards this, in December 1967 social control over banks was announced to secure a better alignment of the banking system to the needs of economic policy. In 1969, 14 banks with deposits of over Rs. 50 crore were nationalised. This was one of the momentous events that shaped the philosophy of financial sector reforms over the next 15 years or so. Subsequently, the insurance sector was nationalised in 1972, and later six banks with deposits more than Rs. 200 crore as on 14 March 14 1980 were nationalised on 15 April 1980.[30] Efforts towards extension

Table 1	Expansion of commercial bank network					
Month year	**Rural centres**	**Semi-urban centres**	**Urban centres**	**Metropolitan centres / port towns**	**Total**	**Population per bank office**
June 1969	1,443 (17.6)	3,337 (40.8)	1,911 (23.3)	1,496 (18.3)	8,187	65,000
December 1975	6,807 (36.3)	5,598 (29.9)	3,489 (18.6)	2,836 (15.1)	18,730	31,660
December 1980	15,105 (46.6)	8,122 (25.1)	5,178 (16.0)	4,014 (12.4)	32,419	20,481
December 1985	30,185 (58.7)	9,816 (19.1)	6,578 (12.8)	4,806 (9.4)	51,385	14,381
December 1990	34,791 (58.2)	11,324 (19.0)	8,042 (13.5)	5,595 (9.4)	59,752	13,756

Source: RBI (2008), p. 98.
Note: Figures within parentheses are percentage shares in total.

of banking network, deposit mobilization and credit extension all over India witnessed a number of policy actions, such as introduction of Lead Bank Scheme, formalization of the concept of priority sector and related stipulation of credit floors by commercial banks (1972), prescription of a minimum lending rate on all loans except for the priority sector (1973), stipulations on aggregate credit limit of borrowers in excess of Rs. 10 lakh (1975) and introduction of Service Area Approach (1988) (RBI, 2008). What did bank nationalization achieve? First, there was tremendous extension of banking network. Illustratively, population per bank office came down from 65,000 in 1969 to little less than 14,000 in 1990 (Table 1). It is clear that the banking system expanded rapidly into rural and semi-rural areas, given the fairly detailed branch licensing policy.

Figure 1 and Charts 1 and 2 on rural deposits show that the expansion of banking into rural areas occurred primarily in the decade following nationalization and then plateaued out. The subsequent decline suggests that nationalization may have resulted in inefficient expansion that had to be reversed subsequently. The share of rural credit in total continued to expand for another half a decade because bank nationalization was complemented by directed credit to agriculture (Chart 3). This raises the question whether other policies such as directed credit or interest subsidies for rural/agriculture lending may not have achieved the same objective more efficiently than nationalization!

The impact of extension of banking in general was also visible in growth of bank credit and deposits, which

Figure 1	Shares of rural deposits and credits

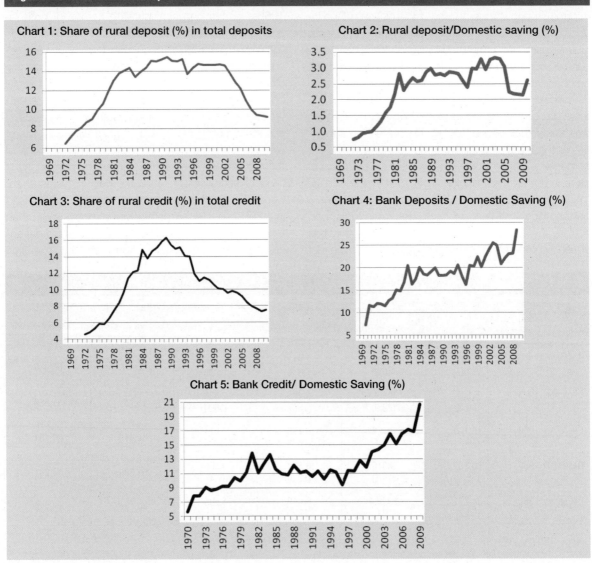

Chart 1: Share of rural deposit (%) in total deposits

Chart 2: Rural deposit/Domestic saving (%)

Chart 3: Share of rural credit (%) in total credit

Chart 4: Bank Deposits / Domestic Saving (%)

Chart 5: Bank Credit/ Domestic Saving (%)

Figure 2   Saving Trajectory (percentage of GDP)

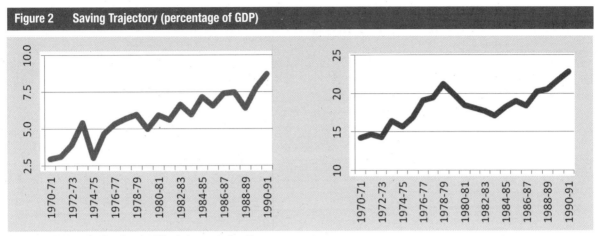

Source: RBI (2011): *Handbook of Statistics on Indian Economy.*

followed the same pattern as that for rural deposit and credit expansion (Charts 4 and 5). Both expanded rapidly in the decade after nationalization, after which deposits plateaued out while credit declined relative to savings. Thus, any impact of nationalization seems to have been limited to one decade. Increased bank branching and deposits were associated with a rise of domestic Indian saving. Gross domestic saving (as a percentage of GDP) increased 14 per cent to nearly 21 per cent over the 1970s but declined in the subsequent decade, confirming that any potential positive effects of nationalization were limited to one decade, while its negative effects emerged gradually and overwhelmed the positive effects during the 1980s. The increase in financial saving (a constituent of household saving) was more sustained – from 3 per cent to nearly

9 per cent (Fig. 2 and Chart 6), probably because of other policies.

Earlier studies have postulated a number of distinct phases in savings behaviour in India (NCAER-EPWRF, 2003; Shetty, 2007). Typically, the low-savings phase of 1950–51 to 1967–68 was followed by a phase of acceleration of savings rate during the next 11 years, viz., 1968–69 through 1983–84 (Table 2).

How far can the increased savings be seen as an outcome of the branch expansion pursued actively after bank nationalization? An issue in this context is the role of other influencing variables. Our own preliminary estimation indicates that even after controlling for variables such as per capita income, growth, interest rate and old age dependency ratio, population per bank branch emerges as a significantly negative variable influencing household savings.[31] That is to say, a fall in population per bank branch tended to have positive influence on household saving rate. This is in tune with similar evidence in the literature (e.g. Athuhorala and Sen, 2004).[32] While such evidence is more symptomatic as to identify the importance of nationalization on domestic savings, a more thorough empirical analysis is needed, with a model containing demographic and macro variables along with a nationalization dummy.[33] Curiously, interest rates often failed to emerge as significant variable influencing saving decisions in India. While this could be indicative of the still existing interest rate restrictions in India (Sahu and Virmani, 2005), such lack of interest rate sensitivity has often been found for developing economies.[34]

Earlier analysts have shown that increased quantum of credit and saving did play an enabling role in promoting capital accumulation and that increases in key financial

Table 2   Phase-wise saving rates

Phases	Periods	Aggregate saving (% of GDP)
1. Low saving phase	17 Years: 1950–51 to 1967–68	11.1
2. Phase of acceleration in savings	11 Years: 1968–69 to 1978–79	16.5
3. Decelerating phase in savings	5 Years: 1979–80 to 1983–84	18.7
4. Recovery phase in saving	12 years: 1985–85 to 1995–96	21.7
5. New high phase	14 Years: 1996–97 to 2009–10	28.6

Source: Shetty (2007), and RBI (2011): *Handbook of Statistics on Indian Economy.*
Note: Due to extension of the last period, taxonomy differs slightly from Shetty (2007).

Figure 3   Increasing pre-emption of commercial banks' resources

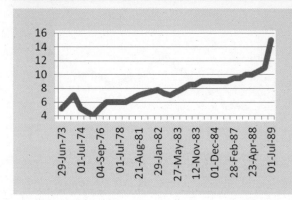

aggregates tended to precede increases in both investment and aggregate output; such an expansion of the financial sector had, however, hardly any influence on total factor productivity in organised manufacturing (Bell and Rousseau, 2001). Thus, in some sense Indian financial development under a government-sponsored regime could be consistent with Gurley and Shaw's (1955) "debt accumulation hypothesis".[35] Despite the positive association,[36] Indian experience of financial development under government auspices did lead to a number of pitfalls. First and foremost, this whole period witnessed a secular increase in cash reserve ratio (CRR) and statutory liquidity ratio (SLR). The CRR was gradually raised from 5.0 per cent in June 1973 to 15.0 per cent by July 1989 and the SLR from 26 per cent in February 1970 to 38.5 per cent in September 1990 (Fig. 3). Thus, by 1991, 53.5 per cent resources of the banking sector were pre-empted in the form of SLR and CRR. Such large pre-emption offered little operational ability of banks and led to crowding-out of private investment from the end-1970s (Fig. 4).

Second, earnings from the pre-empted resources of banks were rather low. However, banks earned less than market rate of interest on eligible CRR balances,

Figure 4   Private credit/total credit (Percentage)

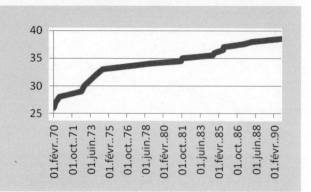

and the yield on government securities was far below the saving deposit interest rates, let alone the lending interest rates. Illustratively, up to 1981–82, yield on government securities was lower than the interest rate paid by banks on deposits of 1 to 3 years' maturity (RBI, 2008). Although the yield on government securities subsequently was raised later, it remained significantly lower than the lending interest rates of banks (Table 3).

Third, as a result of all these, bank profitability was affected adversely and "the proliferation of directed credit arrangements, administered structure of interest rates

Table 3   Structure of interest rates (Percentage)

Year (end-March)	Deposit interest rates			SBI advance rate	Central government securities primary yield
	1 to 3 years	3 to 5 years	More than 5 years		
1971	6.00–6.5	7.0	7.25	7.0-8.5	..
1975	6.75–8.0	7.75–9.0	8.00–10.00	9.0-13.5	5.67
1980	7.0	8.5	10.00	16.5	..
1985	8.00–9.0	10.0	11.00	16.5	9.98
1990	9.00–10.0	10.0	10.00	16.5	11.49

Source: RBI (2008).

Table 4	Return on assets of commercial banks (Percentage)			
Year	SBI	Nationalised banks	Other Indian scheduled commercial banks	Aggregate
1970 (Jan–Dec)	0.48	0.64	0.65	0.59
1975 (Jan–Dec)	1.19	0.57	0.59	0.77
1980 (Jan–Dec)	0.86	0.56	0.59	0.66
1985 (Jan–Dec)	0.08	0.06	0.13	0.07
1989–90 (Apr–Mar)	0.12	0.15	0.23	0.15

Source: RBI (2008).
Note: Return on assets is measured by net profit before tax as a percentage of total assets.

and increase in statutory pre-emptions all had an adverse impact on banks' profitability" (RBI, 2008, p. 106). Deterioration in profitability was more pronounced in respect of the SBI group (Table 4). There is, thus, an influential view that the progress of commercial banking in India at the expense of deterioration in the quality of loan portfolios resulting in sizable non-performing assets (NPAs) declines in productivity and profitability and serious management weaknesses.

After independence and well before banks' nationalization, a number of development finance institutions such as Industrial Development Bank of India (IDBI in 1964) or Industrial Finance Corporation of India (IFCI in 1948) were set up, which tried to fill the gaps in project financing.[37] These institutions provided financial assistance in the form of term loans, underwriting/direct subscription to shares/debentures and guarantees. There has been a secular increase in the disbursements of FIs (Table 5). As a percentage of GDP, disbursements by FIs rose from 0.5 per cent in the first-half of the 1970s to 1.4 per cent in the first-half of the 1980s. Resources mobilised by mutual funds, which were just 0.04 per cent of GDP (at

Table 5	Disbursements of financial institutions and resource mobilization by mutual funds (Percentage of GDP)	
	Total disbursements of FIs	Resources mobilised by mutual funds
1970–71 to 1974–75	0.5	0.04
1975–76 to 1979–80	0.8	0.06
1980–81 to 1984–85	1.4	0.13
1985–86 to 1989–90	1.9	0.75
1989–90 (Apr–Mar)	0.12	0.15

Source: RBI (2008).

current market prices) during the first half of the 1980s increased to 0.75 per cent during the second half of the 1980s. Nevertheless, there were issues of viability of both these types of institutions. Financial institutions got cheap credit from the Government and the RBI via allocation of profits to various long-term operations funds; similarly, high interest rates offered by the Unit Trust of India put undue pressure on the Exchequer. Without belittling their contribution to the Indian economy during the 1970s and 1980s, it may be mentioned that continuance of the financing patterns of these institutions became difficult towards the end of the 1980s.

2. Financial Markets

In terms of financial markets, developments in money, bond and forex market was rather limited till mid-1980s. Call money rate was, for a large period, controlled. There was large recourse to deficit financing by the Government through ad hoc Treasury bills. Thus, auction-based market for Treasury bills or government securities was non-existent and there was hardly any corporate bond market.

Capital market was, however, an exception as India had one of the oldest stock exchanges in Asia with Bombay Stock Exchange having been established in 1875. In fact, Indian capital markets played a major role in the mobilization of savings in the 1950s. Nevertheless, their importance diminished considerably during the 1970s and 1980s; in fact, despite the increase in domestic savings, funds raised from the capital market reduced from 13 per cent of net domestic savings in the 1950s to less than 1 per cent in late 1970s and further to 0.4 per cent in the 1980s (Khambata and Khambata, 1989). There are three potential reasons for this, which need careful empirical investigation: (a) Unreasonable and excessive controls on floatation of a new issue by the Controller of Capital Issues (COCI) and over capital market regulation, particularly for "non-priority" sectors, choked the supply of equity. (b) The subsidy for long-term credit provided through the development finance institutions to "priority credit" made it unprofitable to use the capital market route. (c) The monopoly of the Unit Trust of India (UTI) in the establishment and operation of domestic mutual funds slowed funds inflow into the capital market.

3.   External Account

The thrust of the economic model underlying the planning process in the Indian economy was perceived as "self-reliance", which got translated in terms of an "import substituting" rather than "export promoting" strategy of industrialization. Thus, regarding external sector, this gave rise to three key features of the Indian economy: (a) Investments were financed almost wholly through domestic saving with marginal role of foreign flows. (b) There was reluctance to permit foreign investments or private commercial flows in general. (c) There was almost total reliance on official, especially multilateral, flows, mainly on concessional terms, including recourse to IMF facilities to meet extraordinary situations such as the drought in the 1960s, oil shock of late 1970s and an Extended Fund Facility (EFF) in the 1980s. Thus, till 1980s, external financing was primarily confined to external assistance through multilateral and bilateral sources, mostly on concessional terms to or through the Government (Reddy, 1998).

During most of this period, there was an elaborate structure of exchange controls and in general the external sector was governed by Foreign Exchange Regulation Act, 1973. The objective of exchange controls was primarily to regulate the demand for foreign exchange for various purposes, within the limit set by the available supply. With the breakdown of the Bretton Woods System in 1971, rupee was effectively linked to US dollar. To overcome the weaknesses associated with a single currency peg and to ensure exchange rate stability, with effect from September 1975, rupee was pegged to a basket of currencies. The currency selection and weights assigned were left to the discretion of the RBI and were kept confidential. Interestingly, "the strict control on foreign exchange transactions through the Foreign Exchange Regulations Act (FERA) had resulted in one of the largest and most efficient parallel markets for foreign exchange in the world, i.e. the *hawala* (unofficial) market" (RBI, 2007).

Although export growth accelerated during the second half of the 1980s (from about 4.3 per cent of GDP

in 1987–88 to about 5.8 per cent of GDP in 1990–91), trade imbalances persisted at around 3 per cent of GDP. In 1990–91, these trade imbalances were accompanied by a fall in private remittances, travel and tourism earnings and consequent widening of current account deficit to 3.2 per cent of GDP in 1990–91. Capital flows also dried up during the Gulf crisis of 1990–91, and India had forex reserves barely capable of financing three weeks' imports. All these led to the adoption of exceptional corrective steps, including mortgaging of gold to the Bank of England and taking a loan under a stand-by arrangement from the IMF. Against this backdrop, India embarked on stabilization and structural reforms in early 1990s.[38]

To sum up, while the financial development under Government auspices built up banking network, perhaps giving fillip to financial saving and thereby boosting growth, it was saddled with a number of problems. Heavy segmentation of markets, inefficient use of credit, poor bank profitability, rigidity and lack of competition and efficiency were some of them. By mid-1980s, the Indian policy circles became aware that the financial sector needed to be liberalised for financing a higher growth trajectory, of course, without necessarily sacrificing equity considerations.[39]

C. Financial Liberalization since 1990: Institutions and Markets

One of the early attempts at financial change was The Committee to Review the Working of the Monetary System (Chairman: Sukhamoy Chakravarty; RBI, 1986; Chakravarty Committee hereafter), which recommended developing Treasury bills as a dominant monetary instrument to build up open market operations. Chakravarty Committee also suggested upward revision in the yield structure of Government securities to limit the degree of monetization of budget deficit. The money market in India, however, was underdeveloped till the mid-1980s – dominated by a few large lenders (LIC and UTI) and a large number of borrowers (commercial banks) with a ceiling of 10 per cent on the call money rate. Subsequently, the Working Group on the Money Market (Chairman: N. Vaghul; RBI, 1987) made a number of recommendations to achieve a phased decontrol and development of money markets, new 182-day Treasury bills, withdrawal of ceilings on call money rates, new short-term instruments (commercial paper [CPs] and certificates of deposits [CDs]) and establishment of the Discount and Finance House of India

(DFHI). However, while significant deregulation and development of money market took place by late 1980s, the progress in the deregulation of credit, bond, forex and capital markets was rather limited till the early 1990s – so were banks and other FIs. Against this backdrop, this section gives a brief overview of Indian financial sector reforms and assesses their impact and outcome.[40]

Indian financial Liberalization had diverse elements, including measures for operational autonomy of FIs, establishment of newer institutions, introduction of newer instruments, and establishment of prudential norms for the banking sector. The basic approach was, (a) cautious sequencing of reform measures; (b) introduction of mutually reinforcing norms and regulatory reforms; (c) introduction of complementary reforms across sectors (most important, monetary, fiscal and external sector); (d) development of FIs and financial markets (Reddy, 2004).

At this point, it is important to clarify a conceptual issue. While various official committees have recommended various things for financial sector Liberalization, one can, in principle, distinguish between market development and market de-control/Liberalization and between administrative measures affecting nationalised banks and market decontrol for everyone, including private banks and FIs and firms. Only decontrol of private banks and FIs, markets in which private parties operate, and increased competition to benefit users is true Liberalization. From this viewpoint, reports of different committees had varying degrees of recommendations of market Liberalization for private players.

1. Banks

The key reform measures for the banking sector came from reports of two committees both of which were chaired by M. Narasimham, viz., Report of the Committee on Financial System (Reserve Bank of India, 1991; Narasihmam Committee I) and the Report of the Committee on Banking Sector Reforms (Government of India, 1998; Narasihmam Committee II). Narasihmam Committee I was primarily devoted to giving operational freedom to the commercial banking sector, and recommended measures like reduction in the SLR and CRR, eliminating administrative controls on interest rate and phasing out the concessional interest rates for the priority sector, structural reorganizations of the banking sector (including reduction of the actual numbers of public sector banks), establishment of the Asset Reconstruction Fund (ARF) Tribunal (which could take over the proportion of the bad and doubtful debts

from banks), removal of dual control of the RBI and the Banking Division of the Ministry of Finance (so that the RBI becomes the sole regulator), and giving operational autonomy to the banks (Gokarn, 2001).[41] Narasihmam II was devoted to prudential norms and other stability considerations and recommended prudential regulations such as increase in capital adequacy ratio, risk weights to various securities and a review of functions of bank boards to adopt professional corporate strategy. Apart from these measures, a number of legal and institutional measures were undertaken, which included settling up of *Lok Adalats* (people's courts), debt recovery tribunals, asset reconstruction companies, settlement advisory committees, corporate debt restructuring mechanism, enactment of Securitization and Reconstruction of Financial Assets and Enforcement of Securities Interest (SARFAESI), Act for ensuring creditors' rights, setting up of Credit Information Bureaus for information sharing on defaulters as also other borrowers (Mohan, 2009). Where did all these measures lead to? Let us find the outcomes.

(a) Interest Rate Deregulation

With interest rate deregulation, interest rates have come down in general (Table 6). The administered interest rate structure was rather complex; there have been conscious efforts since 1990 towards its rationalization so as to ensure price discovery and transparency in loan pricing system. Rationalization culminated in almost complete deregulation of lending rates in October 1994, and lending rates of scheduled commercial banks for credit limits of over Rs. 2 lakh were freed and a system of prime lending rate (PLR) was introduced in 1994 (RBI, 2009). Subsequently, a system of Benchmark Prime Lending Rate (BPLR) was introduced in 2003; it was expected to serve as a benchmark rate for banks' pricing of their loan products to ensure that it truly reflected the actual cost. However, since the BPLR system has fallen short of its original objective of bringing transparency to lending rates, a RBI Working Group recommended introduction of a system of base rate which would include (a) card interest rate on retail deposit (deposits below Rs. 15 lakh) with one-year maturity adjusted for current account and savings account deposits; (b) adjustment on account of negative carry in respect of CRR and SLR; (c) un-allocable overhead cost for banks; and (d) average return on net worth. Interest rate deregulation is still on. In this context, the October 2011 Monetary Policy announced deregulation of the savings bank deposit interest rate, a rate that had been regulated so far.

Table 6	Structure of interest rates (Percentage)					
Year	Call money rates	Deposit interest rates			SBI advance rate	Memo: inflation rate
		1 to 3 years	3 to 5 years	Above 5 years		
1990–91	15.85	9.00–10.00	11.00	11.00	16.50	10.3
1995–96	17.73	12.00	13.00	13.00	16.50	8.0
1996–97	7.84	11.00–12.00	12.00–13.00	12.50–13.00	14.50	4.6
1997–98	8.69	10.50–11.00	11.50–12.00	11.50–12.00	14.00	4.4
1998–99	7.83	9.00–11.00	10.50–11.50	10.50–11.50	12.00–14.00	5.9
1999–2000	8.87	8.50–9.50	10.00–10.50	10.00–10.50	12.00	3.3
2000–01	9.15	8.50–9.50	9.50–10.00	9.50–10.00	11.50	7.2
2005–06	5.60	6.00–6.50	6.25–7.00	6.25–7.00	10.25	4.5
2009–10	—	6.00–7.00	6.50–7.50	6.50–7.50	11.75	3.8
2010–11	4.51	8.25–9.00	7.75–9.50	7.75–9.50	8.25	9.6

Source: RBI (2011): *Handbook of Statistics on Indian Economy*.

Notwithstanding deregulation of interest rates, banks tend to face stiff competition from small savings deposit schemes operated by the post offices (OECD, 2011).[42] Typically, postal deposits tend to pull deposits away during the economic downturns (Fig. 5). A recent Government Committee has probed the issues

Figure 5	Estimated margin between small savings and money market interest rates

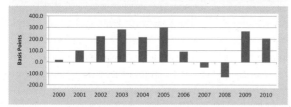

Source: OECD (2011).
Note: The differential is measured as the yield on a one-year small savings deposits relative to the three-month interbank bid price.

relating to viability of the postal deposits schemes and recommended discontinuation of the popular *Kisan Vikas Patra*, where deposit doubles in 8 years 7 months (Government of India, 2011). Figures 4 and 5 show that there was a kind of "J curve effect" (Virmani, 2005) of banking reforms.[43] Reforms on deposit and credit growth in the early 1990s had little or no effect. Only in the late 1990s/early 2000s, increasing amount of domestic savings started being channelled through banks, and the ratio of deposits to domestic savings (Chart 4) and credit to domestic savings (Chart 5) started rising.

(b) Reduction in Statutory Pre-emption

Both CRR and SLR have been reduced over the years. By August 2003 the CRR was reduced to 4.5 per cent and by October 1997 the SLR was reduced to its statutory minimum level of 25 per cent (Fig. 6). Simultaneously, since the automatic moneti-

Figure 6	Freeing of statutory pre-emption of commercial banks' resources (1990 – 2010)

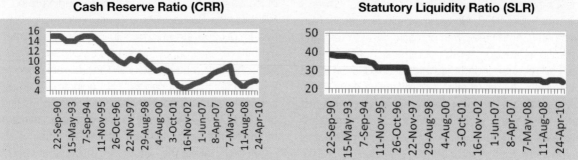

Source: RBI (2011): *Handbook of Statistics on Indian Economy.*
Note: Both CRR and SLR are percentages of domestic net demand and time liabilities.

zation of deficit financing was done away with through agreements between the RBI and the Government of India, SLR emerged as a genuine and prudential tool to ensure safety of the banking system. These reductions boosted the lendable resources of commercial banks. This in turn was reflected in the share of credit going to the private sector.

(c)   Prudential Measures and Health of Indian Banking

There have been a series of prudential measures on the Indian banking system. Given the primacy of capital, capital to risk-weighted assets ratio (CRAR) was stipulated in line with international norms in 1992–93. The CRAR stipulations had been gradually increased, especially in the case of domestic banks, from 4 per cent during 1992–93 to 9 per cent in 1999–2000. The CRAR of the banking system, as at end-March 2010, worked out to 13.6 per cent of assets, far above the stipulated 9 per cent (Table 7). The CRAR of Indian banks under Basel I framework, which had been on a steady rise since 2007, stood at 13.2 per cent at end-March 2009. Under Basel II, CRAR of Indian banks as at end-March 2009 stood at 14.0 per cent, far above the minimum ratio of 9 per cent stipulated by the RBI. This signified that Indian banks successfully managed to meet the increased capital requirement under the changed framework.

Besides, there has been a marked improvement in the quality of banks' balance sheets. Over the last decade, while the banking sector's gross NPAs came down from nearly 15 per cent to less than 3 per cent (both as percentage of total gross advances), in terms of net NPAs the reduction is more significant – from more than 7 per cent to around 1 per cent (Table 7).

Table 7	Non-performing assets and capital position of Indian banking		
	Gross NPAs (as % of gross advances)	Net NPAs (as % of net advances)	CRAR (%)
1998–99	14.7	7.6	11.3
1999–00	12.7	6.8	11.1
2000–01	11.4	6.2	11.4
2004–05	5.2	2.0	12.8
2009–10	2.4	1.1	13.6

Source: RBI (2008).

(d)   Ownership Structure of Indian Banking

Indian banking sector was freshly opened to private sector banking in 1993 and 10 new banks were set up in the private sector; subsequently two new banks after the 2001 revised guidelines.[44] Indian banking sector's basic character continued to remain public, and improved capitalization of public sector banks was initially met by infusion of funds by the government to recapitalise public sector banks. Nevertheless, cumulatively, government fund infusion into the public sector banks since the initiation of reforms for recapitalization amounted to less than 1 per cent of India's GDP, a figure much lower than that for comparator countries (Mohan, 2004). Subsequently, public sector banks have accessed capital markets through issue of equity subject to the maintenance of 51 per cent public ownership. Twenty out of the 27 public sector banks have raised capital from the market (Table 8). More recently, the Government set aside Rs. 165 billion for the recapitalization of public sector banks in the 2010–11 Budget on top of Rs. 31 billion used in two previous Budgets (OECD, 2011).

Nevertheless, due to the entry of new banks and an increase in the share of private banks, the degree of concentration has declined in the banking sector. Interestingly, public sector banks have a tendency to "overinvest" in government securities. Several explanations are offered – The operating cost of these investments is lower and there is no risk of default; besides, during decline in interest rate banks could book trading profits on such investments (Gupta *et al.*, 2011).

There have been some recent policy initiatives regarding entry of new private sector banks in India. Based on the views/comments on a discussion paper on "Entry of New Banks in the Private Sector" (released on 11 August 2010), the RBI released the Draft Guidelines for "Licensing of New Banks in the Private Sector" on 29 August 2011 (RBI had sought further comments on these draft guidelines). Key features of the draft guidelines are

- **Eligible promoters**: Entities/groups in the private sector, owned and controlled by residents, with diversified ownership, sound credentials and integrity and having successful track record of at least 10 years will be eligible to promote banks.[46]
- **Corporate structure**: New banks will be set up only through a wholly owned Non-Operative

Table 8	Ownership structure of public sector banks		
No	Name of the bank	Share of government and RBI (%)	Share of others (%)
1	Bank of Baroda	57.0	43.0
2	Union Bank of India	57.1	42.9
3	Vijaya Bank	57.7	42.3
4	Allahabad Bank	58.0	42.0
5	Andhra Bank	58.0	42.0
6	Oriental Bank of Commerce	58.0	42.0
7	Punjab National Bank	58.0	42.0
8	Dena Bank	58.0	42.0
9	Corporation Bank	58.5	41.5
10	State Bank of India	59.4	40.6
11	IDBI Bank Ltd.	65.1	34.9
12	Bank of India	65.9	34.1
13	Indian Overseas Bank	65.9	34.1
14	Canara Bank	67.7	32.3
15	UCO Bank	68.1	31.9
16	Syndicate Bank	69.5	30.5
17	Bank of Maharashtra	79.2	20.8
18	Indian Bank	80.0	20.0
19	Central Bank of India	80.2	19.8
20	Punjab & Sind Bank	82.1	17.9
21	United Bank of India	85.5	14.5

Source: Mohan (2004) and Reserve Bank of India.

Holding Company (NOHC) to be registered with the RBI as a non-banking finance company (NBFC) which will hold the bank as well as all the other financial companies in the promoter group.

- **Minimum capital requirement**: Minimum capital requirement will be Rs. 500 crore. NOHC shall hold minimum 40 per cent of the paid-up capital of the bank for five years from the date of licensing of the bank.[47]
- **Foreign shareholding**: The aggregate non-resident shareholding in the new bank shall not exceed 49 per cent for the first 5 years after which it will be as per the extant policy.
- Corporate governance: At least 50 per cent of the directors of the NOHC should be independent directors. The corporate structure should not impede effective supervision of the bank and the NOHC on a consolidated basis by the Reserve Bank.[48]

2. Development Financial Institutions

In India, development finance institutions (DFIs) have been an important source of long-term funds (mainly debt) for industry compared with bank loans or other sources of debt. For the Indian corporate sector, it has been found that that DFI lending is not governed by considerations of lobbying, precedence or even to sponsor particular types of projects that might be socially desirable but not privately profitable; rather, the primary role of DFIs has been to reduce financial constraints faced by firms (Bhandari et al., 2003).[49]

As low-cost subsidised funds dried up (from RBI's long-term operations funds) for the FIs, they faced serious fund constraints. Simultaneously, with banks entering the domain of term lending and FIs making a foray into disbursing short-term loans, competition for supply of funds has also increased (Reddy, 2004). Besides, FIs have also entered various fee-based services such as stock-broking, merchant banking, or advisory services. Thus, FIs were forced to change their operations. Industrial Credit and Investment Corporation of India Ltd. (ICICI), a leading FI, turned itself into a full-fledged bank through a reverse-merger with its banking arm ICICI Bank in October 2001 and emerged as the second largest financial service company in India. In September 1994, the IDBI set up IDBI Bank Ltd., in association with SIDBI. In July 1995 came out the public issue of the bank, after which the Government's shareholding came down (though it still retains majority of the shareholding in the bank). Subsequently, the parent body, the Industrial Development Bank of India Ltd., was merged with the IDBI Bank in 2005. While the new entity continues its development finance role, it provides an array of wholesale and retail banking products.

3. Mutual Funds

The mutual fund industry in India started in 1963 with the formation of UTI, at the initiative of the Government of India and Reserve Bank of India. Till 1987, the UTI was the only mutual fund. Year 1987 marked the entry of non-UTI, public sector mutual funds set up by public sector banks and Life Insurance Corporation of India (LIC) and General Insurance Corporation of India (GIC). Subsequently, in 1993, private sector mutual funds were allowed. In February 2003, follow-

Table 9	Net resources mobilised by mutual funds (Rs. Crore)				
Year	UTI	Bank-sponsored mutual funds	FI-sponsored mutual funds	Private sector mutual funds	Total (2 to 5)
1990–91	4553	2352	604	..	7509
1995–96	-6314	113	235	133	-5833
2000–01	322	249	1273	9292	11136
2005–06	3424	5365	2112	41581	52482
2008–09	-3659	4489	5954	-31425	-24641
2009–10	15653	9855	4871	48166	78545

Source: Reserve Bank of India

ing the repeal of the Unit Trust of India Act 1963, the UTI was bifurcated into two separate entities (a Specified Undertaking of the Unit Trust of India representing broadly, the assets of US 64 scheme, assured return and certain other schemes. The second is the UTI Mutual Fund, sponsored by several public sector banks and the LIC. It is registered with SEBI and functions under the Mutual Fund Regulations. Net resources mobilised by mutual funds registered a secular increase (Table 9).

4. Non-Bank Financial Companies

Non-banking financial companies (NBFCs) in India offer a wide variety of financial services and play an important role in providing credit to the unorganised sector and small borrowers at the local level. Various types of NBFCs exist, such as, equipment-leasing companies, hire purchase companies and loan and investment companies. In terms of relative importance of various activities financed by NBFCs, hire-purchase finance is the largest activity, accounting for over one-third of their total assets, followed by loans and inter-corporate deposits, equipment leasing and investment. In terms of public deposit taking activities, residuary non-banking companies (RNBCs), which bear some similarity to banks in terms of asset composition, hold the largest deposits. The spate of reforms touched NBFCs as well. In light of legal amendments in 1997, the regulatory focus of NBFCs was redefined. While NBFCs accepting public deposits have been subject to the entire gamut of regulations, those not accepting public deposits have been sought to be regulated in a limited manner.

5. Insurance

The process of re-opening of the insurance sector began in early 1990s. In 1993, the Government set up a committee under the chairmanship of former RBI Governor R.N. Malhotra to look into reforming the insurance sector. The committee submitted its report in 1994 recommending that the private sector be permitted to enter the insurance industry. In particular, the committee proposed that that foreign companies be allowed to enter by floating Indian companies, preferably a joint venture with Indian partners. However, there was strong political resistance, and it was only in 2000 that the law was amended to allow private sector insurance companies, with foreign equity allowed up to 26 per cent, to enter the field (Ahluwalia, 2002). The Insurance Regulatory and Development Authority (IRDA) was constituted as an autonomous body to regulate and develop the insurance industry and has been incorporated as a statutory body in April 2000. In December 2000, GIC subsidiaries were restructured as independent companies and at the same time GIC was converted into a national re-insurer. Parliament passed a bill de-linking the four subsidiaries from GIC in July 2002. Today, 24 general insurance companies and 23 life insurance companies operate in the country. The extension of insurance network is reflected in significant increase in insurance penetration and density (Table 10).

6. Financial Markets [53]

Having looked into the institutional structure of financial system in India, we now turn to financial markets. For the sake of completeness, one can delve into five such markets: (a) money, (b) credit, (c) bonds (G-sec and corporate bonds), (d) forex and (e) stock/equity. Admittedly, each segment has a specific function to do; for example, while money market tries to meet mismatches in temporary short-term liquidity, short-term working capital of the corporate is met through money market. Of these, credit market has already been covered under banking sector reforms; so we concentrate on the other four markets. A key feature about the Indian financial sector needs to be noted first. Currently, the corporate sector in India raises its resources through a variety of resources – banks and non-banks, domestic and foreign sources. Illustratively, in 2009–10 out of the total flow of resources nearly 55 per cent came from non-banks and more than 20 per cent from foreign resources (such as, FDI, FII

Table 10	Insurance penetration and density in India					
Year	Life		Non-life		Total	
	Density (US $)	Penetration (%)	Density (US $)	Penetration (%)	Density (US $)	Penetration (%)
2001	9.1	2.15	2.4	0.56	11.5	2.71
2002	11.7	2.59	3.0	0.67	14.7	3.26
2003	12.9	2.26	3.5	0.62	16.4	2.88
2004	15.7	2.53	4.0	0.64	19.7	3.17
2005	18.3	2.53	4.4	0.61	22.7	3.14
2006	33.2	4.10	5.2	0.60	38.4	4.80
2007	40.4	4.00	6.2	0.60	46.6	4.70
2008	41.2	4.00	6.2	0.60	47.4	4.60
2009	47.7	4.60	6.7	0.60	54.3	5.20

Source: IRDA, India (2010), Annual Report, 2009–10.
Notes: (1) Insurance density is measured as ratio of premium (in US dollars) to total population.
(2) Insurance penetration is measured as ratio of premium (in US dollars) to GDP (in US dollars).

Table 11	Flow of Financial Resources to the Commercial Sector			
Sources	2009–10		2010–11	
	Amount (Rs. crore)	Share (%)	Amount (Rs. crore)	Share (%)
1. Financial resources from banks	478,614	44.8	711,031	58.2
(a) Non-food credit	466,960	43.7	681,501	55.8
(b) Non-SLR investment by SCBs	11,654	1.1	29,530	2.4
2. Financial resources from non-banks (2a+2b)	588,784	55.2	511,006	41.8
(a) Domestic sources	365,214	34.2	292,084	23.9
1. Public issues by non-financial entities	31,956	3.0	28,520	2.3
2. Gross private placements by non-financial entities	141,964	13.3	63,947	5.2
3. Net issuance of CPs subscribed to by non-banks	26,148	2.4	17,207	1.4
4. Net credit by housing finance companies	28,485	2.7	38,386	3.1
5. Accommodation by the four RBI regulated AIFI	33,783	3.2	40,007	3.3
6. Systemically important non-deposit taking NBFCs	60,663	5.7	67,937	5.6
7. LIC's gross investment in corporate debt etc	42,215	4.0	36,080	3.0
(b) Foreign sources	223,570	20.9	218,922	17.9
1. External commercial borrowings	15,674	1.5	52,899	4.3
2. ADR/GDR issues excluding banks and FIs	15,124	1.4	9,248	0.8
3. Short-term credit from abroad	34,878	3.3	50,177	4.1
4. FDI to India	157,894	14.8	106,598	8.7
3. Total flow of resources (1+2)	1,067,398	100.0	1,222,037	100.0

Source: Reserve Bank of India.

or ADR) (Table 11). Thus, the Indian financial system cannot be now called a closed bank-based system. Indian corporates have been innovative enough to utilize instruments such as CPs, and the Indian financial system has also been original enough to supply such products. Following is a quick rundown of reforms in the four key constituents of financial markets in India.

(a) Money Market

The sub-segments of the money market are rather diverse and cover instruments as wide as call money, Treasury bills, CP, CDs, repo or collateralised borrowing and lending obligations (CBLO). Reforms in call money market emerged as a pure-money market which only banks access to meet their liquidity shortfalls, and the call rate emerges as an effective operating target of monetary policy whereby the call rate is purported to be kept within the corridor of repo and reverse repo rate of the RBI (Fig. 7).[54] As the call money market is essentially for banks, a new product called the CBLO was introduced in January 2003. With key players as banks, FIs, insurance companies, mutual funds, non-bank financial companies, Provident and Pension Funds, CBLO has emerged as a major money market discounted instrument, and its transaction volume, accounting for more than 60 per cent of aggregate transaction in money market, has far surpassed call money volumes.[55] Another facility for non-banks to manage their short-term liquidity mismatches is market repo. These apart, CP was introduced as a low-cost alternative to bank loans in January 1990 and CDs were introduced in 1989 as a short-term unsecured promissory note with maturity period ranging from 15 days to 365 days for banks. Currently, the money market is fairly diverse and serves various players, depending on the tenor and risk appetite.

Figure 7   Repo, Reverse Repo and Call Money Rates

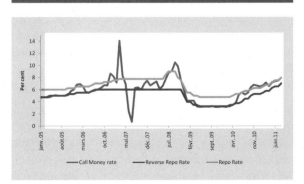

There is evidence of increasing integration between Indian and global money market. Illustratively, it has been found that the short-term (up to three months) money markets in India are getting progressively integrated with those in the United States even though the degree of integration is far from perfect and that covered interest parity is found to hold for while uncovered interest parity fails to hold (Bhatt and Virmani, 2005).[56]

(b) Bond Market

As already indicated bond market comprises two dissimilar segments: G-Sec and corporate bonds. We will deal with them separately. Issuing fixed coupon G-Secs was done away with in the initial phase of reform and a system of auctions was introduced in 1992 for Central Government securities, which signalled the transition to a market-related interest rate system. The abolition of automatic monetization through *ad hoc* Treasury bills and the introduction of Ways and Means Advances (WMA) system in April 1997 provided greater market orientation for government securities. While the RBI continued to absorb government securities through devolvement/private placements, these were essentially market driven and were conducted to offload them in the market when the liquidity conditions stabilise. This was indeed in sharp contrast to the *de facto* 'privately fixed private placement' in the era of the *ad hoc* Treasury Bills, which virtually left little manoeuvrability for the conduct of monetary policy (RBI, 2007). Since the inception of the auction system, multiple-price auction system has been used for dated securities. The uniform price auction format, followed for the issuance of 91-day Treasury bills in November 1998, was extended to auctions of Central Government dated securities on a selective basis from 2001. Unlike Central Government market borrowings, a predominant share of State Government market borrowings was conducted by way of tap issues up to 2005–06. Thus, with significant increase in turnover and elongation of the maturity period, the G-Sec market has undergone radical transformation during last 20 years (Table 12).

In terms of institutional development, establishment of the Clearing Corporation of India Limited (CCIL) and primarily dealers are major initiatives in the bond market. CCIL was set up in April 2001 to provide exclusive clearing and settlement for transactions in money, GSecs and foreign exchange. The prime objective was to improve efficiency in the transac-

Table 12   Progress of the Indian G-Sec market

	1992	1996	2003	2009
1. Outstanding stock (Rs. in billions)	769	1375	6739	13589
2. Outstanding stock as ratio of GDP (per cent)	14.7	14.2	27.3	25.5
3. Turnover/GDP (per cent)	—	34.2	202.9	332.6
4. Average maturity of the securities issued during the year (in years)	—	5.7	15.3	13.8
5. Weighted average cost of the securities issued during the year (per cent)	11.8	13.8	7.3	7.7
6. Minimum and maximum maturities of stock issued during the year (years)	N.A.	2–10	7–30	4–30
7. PDs' share in the turnover a. Primary market b. Secondary market	— —	— —	65.1 21.7	45.4 18.8
8. Transactions on CCIL (face value Rs. in billions)	—	—	15,323	62,545

Source: Mohan and Ray (2009), p. 160.
Note: 1. Outstanding stock represents the total market loans of Central Government.
2. Turnover is the total of outright and repo turnover in Central G-Secs.
3. Outright turnover and repo turnover are calculated as twice and four times the transactions volume, respectively.
4. Data exclude devolvement but include MSS and non-competitive bids.

tion settlement process, insulate the financial system from shocks emanating from operation-related issues and undertake other related activities that would help broaden and deepen money, debt and forex markets. It commenced operations on 15 February 2002 when the RBI's Negotiated Dealing System (NDS) went live. Primary Dealers (PDs) came into existence in 1996 to support the Government's market borrowing program and improve the secondary market liquidity in government securities. PDs were also expected to encourage voluntary holding of government securities among investors. The PD system has created institutions whose basic interest is not to hold G-Secs but to participate in primary auctions to acquire securities and to use them in secondary market operations. PDs have access to the liquidity adjustment facility (LAF) of the RBI.[58]

In some sense, developments in corporate debt market were less spectacular than the progress in G-Sec market. Before the reform period, the corporate bond market was dormant on account of control on interest rates for corporate bonds as well as limited issuances. With the abolition of interest rate ceiling for corporate bonds in May 1992, the corporate debt market was given the initial vibrancy. Major reforms have started in the corporate bond market following the recommendation of the High Level Committee on Corporate Bonds and Securitization on corporate debt market in India (Government of India, 2005; Chairman: R H Patil). The Committee made a number of recommendations relating to rationalising the

primary issuance procedure, facilitating exchange trading, increasing the disclosure and transparency standards and strengthening the clearing and settlement mechanism in secondary market. Based on the recommendations of the Patil Committee, SEBI and RBI have taken various measures to develop the corporate bond market in India, such as SEBI's approval to launch trade reporting platforms by BSE, NSE and FIMMDA and the RBI permitting repos in corporate bonds. FII limit for investment in domestic corporate bonds has recently been raised to US$40 billion, of which US$25 billion is for investment in infrastructure bonds with a residual maturity of over five years. Investments in such bonds shall have a minimum lock-in period of three years. Recently, the 2011–12 Union Budget exempted bonds issued by Infrastructure Development Funds from withholding tax. In recent years, the corporate bond market has shown significant growth in terms of outstanding stock and volumes traded in the secondary market (Table 13). Much of the volume increase has come in the OTC segment of the corporate bonds as reported in the Fixed Income, Money and Derivatives Market (FIMMDA) platform.

However, the market is still underdeveloped and illiquid. Illiquidity in the corporate bond market can primarily be attributed to the corporates' apparent preference to finance their requirements through private placement and external borrowing by large issuers. The success of the measures taken by regulators is contingent on the markets' response to them. For instance, although FII limits on debt flows have been periodically raised, actual flows are below the sanctioned limit. Despite the guidelines for repos on corporate bonds having been issued more than a year ago, there are very few transactions where corporate bonds are used as the underlying.

(c) Foreign Exchange Market

The approach to foreign exchange management policy was transformed starting with the introduction of Partial Convertibility of rupee in 1992 (termed LERMS by the RBI, which operationalised the concept) and near convertibility under a managed float in 1993 [Virmani (1992a,b,c), (2001) (2003)]. Simultaneously, a new conceptual approach to foreign exchange policy and management was developed, which culminated in the replacement of The Foreign Exchange Regulation Act (FERA), 1973, with the Foreign Exchange Management Act (FEMA), 1999.[59] The regulatory reform efforts by RBI in the forex market were based on more detailed reports such as those by the Expert Group on Foreign Exchange Markets in India (Chairman: O. P. Sodhani; RBI, 1995). Sodhani Committee identified various regulations inhibiting the growth of the market and recommended measures, such as, permitting firms to hedge their foreign exchange exposure, or allowing the banks to fix their own exchange position limits such as intra-day and overnight limits. The Group recommended various other short-term and long-term measures to activate and facilitate market functioning and promote the development of a vibrant derivative market (RBI, 2007).

Under FEMA, the RBI delegated powers to authorised dealers (ADs) to release foreign exchange for a variety of purposes. The rupee–foreign currency swap was allowed and additional hedging instruments such as foreign currency–rupee options, cross-currency options, interest rate swaps (IRS) and currency swaps, caps/collars and forward rate agreements (FRAs) were introduced. The draft comprehensive guidelines of 20 April 2007 for accounting and valuation of derivatives provided a holistic framework for regulating the derivatives business of banks. Users such as importers and exporters having crystallised un-hedged exposure in respect of current account transactions can now write covered call and put options in both foreign currency/rupee and cross-currency and receive premia, and market makers may write cross-currency options. Besides, market makers may offer plain vanilla American foreign currency–rupee options. At present, the forex market is divided into two segments: over-the-counter (OTC) market (including spot, forwards and swaps) and exchange-traded currency futures.

The *BIS Triennial Central Bank Survey of Foreign Exchange and Derivatives Market Activity, 2010*, estimated that the percentage share of the rupee in total foreign exchange market turnover covering all currencies increased from 0.3 per cent in 2004 to 0.9 per cent in 2010. Liquidity in the foreign exchange market has increased manifold over the years and the efficiency of the market, as reflected in the narrowing of bid-ask spread for USD–INR rupee, seems to have gone up (Fig. 8). However, still there are issues such as transparency in the currency market from the view point of customers, as banks do not unbundle

Table 13   Secondary market transactions in domestic bonds (Rs. billion)

	Outright transactions in government securities			Transactions in corporate bonds	Total transactions in bonds	Share of corporate bonds in total bonds
	Central government securities	State government securities	Total			
2004–05	8852.2	264.7	9116.9	—	—	—
2005–06	6735.0	200.7	6935.7	—	—	—
2006–07	7566.6	125.5	7692.0	—	—	—
2007–08	14785.4	157.5	14942.8	958.9	15,902	6.0
2008–09	19645.9	352.5	19998.4	1,481.60	21,480	6.9
2009–10	25218.9	764.3	25983.2	4,012.00	29,995	13.4
2010–11	25926.7	483.3	26410.0	6,052.74	32,463	18.6

Source: Reserve Bank and SEBI.

the price on the currency market as opposed to their intermediation fee (Shah *et al.*, 2008).

Figure 8   Market Efficiency: Bid-Ask spread of INR-USD

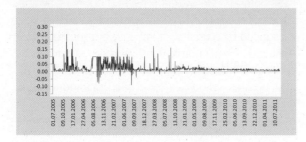

(d)   Stock Market

The Indian equity market has witnessed a series of reforms since early 1990s. SEBI, which was initially set up in April 1988 as a non-statutory body, was given statutory powers in January 1992 for regulating the securities markets. SEBI was given the twin mandate of protecting investors' interests and ensuring the orderly development of the capital market. The most significant reform in respect of the primary capital market was the introduction of free pricing. The Capital Issues (Control) Act, 1947 was repealed in 1992 paving the way for market forces in the determination of pricing of issues and allocation of resources for competing uses. The issuers of securities were allowed to raise capital from the market without requiring any consent from any authority and restrictions on rights and bonus issues were also removed. Institutional development was at the core of the reform process. The setting up of the National Stock Exchange of India Ltd. (NSE) as an electronic trading platform set a benchmark of operating efficiency for other stock exchanges in the country.[60] The establishment of National Securities Depository Ltd. (NSDL) in 1996 and Central Depository Services (India) Ltd. (CSDL) in 1999 has enabled paperless trading in the exchanges. The electronic fund transfer (EFT) facility combined with dematerialization of shares created a conducive environment for reducing the settlement cycle in stock markets.

Trading in derivatives such as stock index futures, stock index options and futures and options in individual stocks was introduced to provide hedging options to the investors and to improve "price discovery" mechanism in the market. Another significant reform has been a move towards corporatization and demutualization of stock exchanges. An important develop-

ment of the reform process was the opening up of mutual funds industry to the private sector in 1992, which earlier was the monopoly of the UTI and mutual funds set up by public sector FIs. Since 1992, foreign institutional investors (FIIs) were permitted to invest in all types of securities subject to some pre-assigned limits. Besides, the Indian corporate sector was allowed to access international capital markets through American Depository Receipts (ADRs), Global Depository Receipts (GDRs), Foreign Currency Convertible Bonds (FCCBs) and External Commercial Borrowings (ECBs). Eligible foreign companies have been permitted to raise money from domestic capital markets through issue of Indian Depository Receipts (IDRs). The stock market over the last two decades has shown considerable buoyancy in its activity levels (Table 14). However, the effect of the 1990s reforms emerged clearly in the 2000s (Fig. 9). The combined value of turnover of the BSE and the NSE exceeds that in many middle-income countries (Malaysia, Thailand, Brazil) and NSE ranks worldwide fifth in terms of turnover in the derivative market (OECD, 2011).

Figure 9:   Market Capitalization of listed companies (Percentage of GDP)

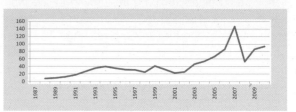

Today, the Indian stock market size is around 70 per cent of the GDP, which is comparable to other emerging market economies. The introduction of exchange traded derivative instruments such as options and futures in 2000 has enabled investors to better hedge their positions and reduce risks. As of April 2011, the NSE trades in futures and options on 224 individual stocks and four stock indices. FIIs have an increasing presence in the equity derivatives markets and currently contribute around 22 per cent of the market turnover. Derivatives on stock indexes and individual stocks have grown rapidly since inception. In particular, Index stock options have become hugely popular, accounting for about 70 per cent of traded value in April 2011.

To sum up, Indian financial markets have undergone reforms of far-reaching significance. Different segments of the markets have shown differing degree of vibrancy and activity. Table 15 describes the average daily turnover in different segments of the Indian financial market.

Table 14   Some stock market indicators and external exposure of Indian corporates

Year	Resources mobilized from the primary market (Rs. crore)	Market capitalization at BSE (Rs. crore)	Market capitalization at NSE (Rs. crore)	ADRs/GDRs (US$ million)	ECBs (US$ million)
1993–94	24,372	3,68,071	NA	1,597	686
1994–95	27,633	4,35,481	3,63,350	2,050	1,124
1995–96	20,804	5,26,476	4,01,459	683	1,284
1996–97	14,284	4,63,915	4,19,367	1,366	2,856
1997–98	4,570	5,60,325	4,81,503	645	4,010
1998–99	5,587	5,45,361	4,91,175	270	4,367
1999–2000	7,817	9,12,842	10,20,426	768	333
2000–01	6,108	5,71,553	6,57,847	831	4,303
2001–02	7,543	6,12,224	6,36,861	477	-1,585
2002–03	4,070	5,72,198	5,37,133	600	-1,692
2003–04	23,272	12,01,207	11,20,976	459	-2,925
2004–05	28,256	16,98,428	15,85,585	613	5,194
2005–06	27,382	30,22,191	28,13,201	2,552	2,508
2006–07	33,508	35,45,041	33,67,350	3,776	16,103
2007–08	87,029	51,38,014	48,58,122	6,645	22,609
2008–09	16,220	30,86,075	28,96,194	1,162	7,941
2009–10	57,555	61,65,619	60,09,173	3,328	2,522

Source: SEBI (2011): *Handbook of Statistics on the Indian Securities Market, 2010.*

Table 15:   Average daily volumes in domestic financial markets (Rs crore)

	March 2010	March 2011
I. Money market		
1. LAF [(-): injection; (+): absorption]	37,640	-80,963
2. Call money	8,812	11,278
3. Market repo	19,150	15,134
4. CBLO	60,006	43,201
5. Commercial paper (Outstanding)	75,506	80,305
6. Certificates of deposit (Outstanding)	3,41,054	4,24,740
II. Bond market		
7. G-Sec	6,621	8,144
8. Corporate bond	1,598	1,314
III. Forex market		
9. Inter-bank (US$ mn)	16,082	22,211
IV. Stock market		
10. Volume in BSE and NSE (cash segment)	9,191	7,276

Source: Reserve Bank of India
Note: Average daily outright trading volume in Central Government dated securities.

D. Capital Account Liberalization

No account of financial sector reform in India is complete without a discussion on capital account Liberalization in India. In fact, much of critiques and perceptions on India's "slow" financial Liberalization stems from the calibrated pace of India's capital account Liberalization.[61] The official stance of the RBI, on the other hand, is that, "the Indian approach to capital account convertibility (CAC) has been one of gradualism, treating Liberalization of the capital account as a continuous process rather than a single event" (RBI, 2004).[62] The Report of the Committee on Capital Account Convertibility (Chairman: S.S. Tarapore), submitted in May 1997, provided the framework for Liberalization of capital account transactions in India. The Committee recommended a phased implementation of CAC in India to be completed by the year 1999–2000 and prescribed the macroeconomic framework for implementing full convertibility in terms of the preconditions for greater Liberalization. Subsequently, in 2006, the Report of the Committee on Fuller Capital Account Convertibility (Chairman: S.S. Tarapore) evaluated the progress of CAC and noted that of three important milestones for reaching CAC, while two (reduction in

Table 16	India's balance of payments: current and capital account (Billions of US$)							
		Capital account						
Year	Current account	Foreign investment	External assistance, net	Commercial borrowing, net	Rupee debt service	NRI deposit, net	Other capital	Total Capital A/C
1990–91	-9.7	0.1	2.2	2.2	-1.2	1.5	2.3	7.2
1995–96	-5.9	4.8	0.9	1.3	-1.0	1.1	-2.4	4.7
2001–02	3.4	8.1	1.2	-1.6	-0.5	2.8	-1.6	8.4
2005–06	-9.9	21.4	1.8	2.8	-0.6	2.8	-3.2	25.0
2009–10	-38.4	65.5	3.3	3.3	-0.1	2.9	-23.1	51.8
2010–11	-44.3	54.8	5.0	11.6	-0.1	3.2	-17.2	57.3

Source: Reserve Bank of India.

inflation and NPAs of the banking sector) have been substantially reached, the third one – reduction of fiscal deficit – is yet to be reached.[63]

What have been the trends in India's current and capital account? While India traditionally maintained a manageable current account deficit (2–3 per cent of GDP), increasingly capital account is financed by foreign investment – both FDI and portfolio. After experiencing a sharp fall during the crisis of 2008–09, net capital flows surged to US$53.6 billion (4.1 per cent of GDP) during 2009–10 (Table 16). Foreign investments have, however, showed considerable volatility.

Another symptom of confidence of the Indian capital account is outward FDI from India (Virmani, 2009). While India has a history of outward FDI dating back to late 1950s, total outflows remained small till early 1990s. While outflows started to increase in the mid-1990s, there has been a surge in outflows since 2005 following significant capital account Liberalization (Fig. 10). Measures such as removal of foreign exchange restrictions on capital transfers for acquisition of foreign ventures by Indian firms have in particular boosted outward FDI from India. With the emergence of a number of Indian corporate as leading multinationals, India's share in total outward FDI of developing countries increased from below 0.5 per cent in early 1990s to nearly 6 per cent in recent years (Athukorala, 2009). India's approach to the capital account has been important in terms of the progress in financial Liberalization. While the capital account has been liberalised in a calibrated manner, in its approach to opening of the capital account, India has clearly recognised a hierarchy in capital flows and has favoured equity flows over debt flows and foreign direct investment over portfolio

investment (Virmani, 2007, 2009b; Mohan and Kapur, 2009).

Figure 10	Outward FDI from India (Million of United States dollars)

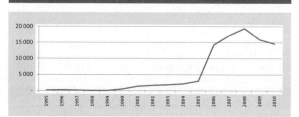

Source: World Investment Report, 2010, UNCTAD

There are several elements of the Indian official policy approach to capital flows (Gopinath, 2011). First, there is an explicitly stated active capital account management framework, based on the policy stance of encouraging non-debt creating and long-term capital inflows and discouraging debt flows. Second, the policy space is wide enough to use multiple instruments – quantitative limits, price based measures as well as administrative measures, particularly for foreign currency borrowing by firms. Third, short-term debt permitted only for trade transaction. Fourth, the "original sin" of excessive foreign currency borrowings by domestic entities, particularly the sovereign, is consciously avoided. Fifth, prudential regulations are used to prevent excessive dollarization of balance sheets of financial sector intermediaries, particularly banks. Sixth, a cautious approach is adopted regarding dollarization of liabilities of domestic entities. Seventh, significant Liberalization has been made of permissible avenues for outward investments for domestic entities.

India's approach towards capital account Liberalization has been calibrated and gradual. The ceiling of investment in Government securities by foreign institutional investors has been increased from US$ 1 billion in 1998 to 5 billion in 2008 – For FII investment in corporate debt securities the ceiling has reached from US$ 0.5 billion in 2004 to US$ 15 billion in 2009. More recently, Government of India increased the investment limit for FIIs in government securities and corporate bonds by $5 billion each. FIIs would be able to invest up to $15 billion in government securities, compared with the current $10 billion and up to $20 billion in corporate bonds, compared with the current $15 billion. Furthermore, the incremental limit of $5 billion can be invested in securities without any residual maturity criterion.

Has capital account Liberalization in India been too little and too slow? While this approach seemed to have served the country well, there are opinions whether a more liberal approach could have been adopted to handle the capital account.[64] Nevertheless, often the discussion of a faster vis-à-vis slower/calibrated capital account Liberalization gets caricatured into extreme positions on merits and pitfalls of a cautious approach. Without being emphatic on one view over the other, following counterfactuals could be considered in this context.[65] First, given the inflation rate and interest rate configuration of India vis-à-vis major financial centres, a cautious approach to debt vis-à-vis a more liberal approach to equity in India seemed to have served the country well. Second, the presence of high fiscal deficit seems to be a drag in the pace of a faster Liberalization in debt market. Third, with the outbreak of the Euro Area Sovereign debt crisis, a cautious policy of domestically held sovereign debt seems to be gaining more support. Fourth, an important feature of the impact of exchange rate on reserve account in India has been its asymmetry in terms of negative and positive shocks, with the former translating more readily into nominal depreciation than the latter do into nominal appreciation (Virmani, 2001, 2003). Finally, notwithstanding the impossibility of simultaneously attaining monetary autonomy, fixed exchange rate and capital mobility, Indian experience seems to show that instead of the corner solutions, the policymaker can devise intermediate outcomes (Joshi, 2003; Virmani, 2007, 2009b; Mohan and Kapur, 2009).

E. Concluding Observations

We started with the question whether the pace of financial Liberalization has served the country well? A description of the different facets of financial develop-

ment during 1970 - 1990 (i.e. prior to financial Liberalization) allows one to discern a basic trend – while credit availability was ensured in the economy the extent of financial repression was often. Thus, it was the quantum effect of financial development without necessarily influencing the price that benefited growth process. The process of financial Liberalization initiated in early 1990s on the other hand was multi-pronged – it concentrated on development of institution, market microstructure, risk mitigating instruments and regulatory and technological infrastructure. In the process, the health and stability of the financial system was improved. In terms of a check while money, G-Sec and equity market improved a lot, there is much to be desired in the corporate debt market. While competition was enhanced among domestic participants, opening up of the financial sector to foreign participants was done a calibrated manner. This calibrated pace of reform ensured safety and stability of the financial system and did not involve policy reversals.

To sum up, financial Liberalization in India improved the allocation of funds and allowed the economy to reap the benefits of static welfare efficiency; but reforms that could increase competitive supply of funds to new entrepreneurs, credit rationed producers and (direct) investors have been somewhat limited. Nevertheless, given the fiscal deficit and inflation configuration, the opening up of the financial sector to foreign players has been calibrated. If there is any lesson from the global financial crisis, it is perhaps better to be measured and safe rather than fast and rash. To say that financial Liberalization is a process and not necessarily an end in itself is a cliché – but such a cliché perhaps describes the true spirit of financial reforms.

How do we see the way forward? A number of recent committees have gone into the issues and offered interesting recommendation. In particular, the Committee on Financial Sector Reforms (Chairman: Raghuram Rajan) have gone into a number of aspects of the financial sector Liberalization. The Committee put forward recommendations spread over diverse areas, such as, adoption of inflation targeting, setting up of a Financial Sector Oversight Agency, allowing greater participation of foreign investors in domestic markets and in particular, steadily opening up investment in the rupee corporate and government bond markets to foreign investors, delinking the banks from additional government oversight, including by the Central Vigilance Commission and the Parliament, freeing banks to set up branches and ATMs anywhere, rewriting of financial sector regulation, strengthening the capacity of the Deposit Insurance and Credit Guarantee Corporation (DICGC). While select recommendations of the committee have already been acted upon (e.g. setting up of the Financial Stability and Development Council (FSDC) under the Chairmanship of the Finance Minister), some of the recommendations of the committee has drawn considerable flak. Illustratively, the Committee's treatment of the "macroeconomic framework" and adoption of inflation targeting has been criticised as, "curiously academic and aloof from the realities of the Indian macroeconomic setting and experience ...there seems to be little understanding of the potential and possibilities of macroeconomic policy in a developing country with an "intermediate" exchange rate regime of managed flexibility and partial capital controls" (Acharya, 2008).[66] Besides, it has been articulated categorically that inflation targeting is neither desirable nor practical in India for a variety of reasons: (a) preference of being guided simultaneously by the objectives of price stability, financial stability and growth rather than a single goal oblivious of the larger development context; (b) predominance of food items (46 - 70 per cent) in the various consumer prices indices and vulnerability to large supply shocks; (c) multiplicity of price indices (one wholesale price index and four consumer price indices); (d) impeded monetary transmission mechanism because of the large fiscal deficits, persistence of administered interest rates and illiquid private bond markets; and (e) need to manage the monetary fall-out of volatile capital flows (Subbarao, 2009).

The ongoing global financial crisis culminating into Euro Area Sovereign Debt crisis has questioned many of the standard lessons of financial Liberalization. While the elusive quest for a new normal is on, the regulatory paradigm of the financial sector is being reformulated all over the world. The potential capability of the financial sector to disrupt economic activity and problems like heavy leverage, complexity of financial products, too-big-to fail FIs, perverse incentive structure in financial sector have all come to the fore towards redesigning financial sector reforms. Naturally, issues regarding pace and sequencing of reforms within the financial sector Liberalization process are being contemplated afresh. Going forward, these issues are likely to shape the contours of Indian financial Liberalization.

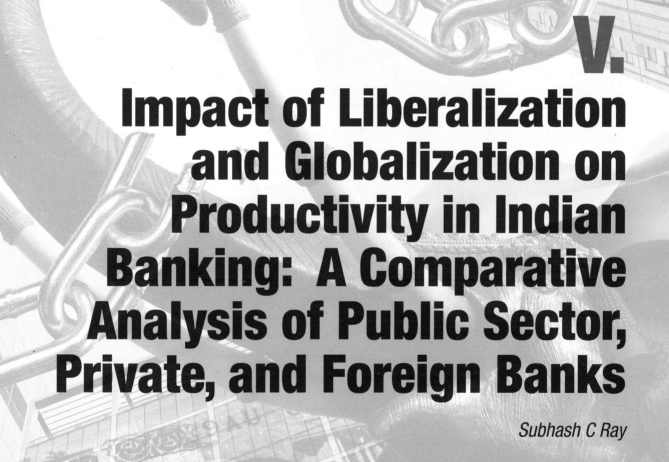

V.

Impact of Liberalization and Globalization on Productivity in Indian Banking: A Comparative Analysis of Public Sector, Private, and Foreign Banks

Subhash C Ray

A. Introduction

In an economy that has been under strict government control over years, the main components of Liberalization are public sector downsizing (if not elimination) creating room for domestic firms and allowing entry of foreign firms. In this respect, Indian banking industry provides an ideal setting for evaluating the impact of Liberalization and removing entry restrictions. India, though dominated by public sector banks, already had a significant presence of private domestic banks and foreign banks. Banking reforms have created a more level playing field where all banks compete within a new set of broad (and far more relaxed) regulations. Data on the performance of the three different categories of banks over the past two decades offer an opportunity to assess to what extent regulatory changes have improved the productive efficiency of the Indian banking sector.

Independent India adopted a strategy of planned economic development assigning a dominant role to the public sector. Financing the huge expenditure on large-scale projects required intermediation of a major share of loanable funds to the public sector principally through banks. This made strict government control of commercial banks almost inevitable. As a first step in this direction, the former Imperial Bank of India was nationalised in 1955 and State Bank of India (SBI) was formed. Subsequently, SBI acquired state-owned banks in eight former princely states in 1959. Another 14 private banks each with deposits over Rs. 500 million were nationalised in 1969. As a result, the share of bank branches under government control increased to 84 per cent. Finally, in 1980, six more private banks with deposits exceeding Rs. 2 billion were nationalised, leaving mere 10 per cent of bank branches under private control.

Rigid regulation ensured that banks offered the government easy and low-cost access to funds and effectively served as channels for implementing the various fiscal policies. Apart from the required cash reserve ratio (CRR) banks were also subjected to statutory liquidity ratio (SLR), which forced them to hold a mandated proportion of their credit in the form of government securities. Not surprisingly, the administered interest rates on these securities were below the market rate. Interest rates on loans and deposits were also strictly regulated by the government instead of being determined by the market. Moreover, since 1969 banks had been required to extend at least 33 per cent of their total credit to the priority sector (consisting of agriculture and small-scale industries), which was not adequately served otherwise. Subsequently the priority sector lending requirement was raised to 40 per cent. Directed lending targeted towards the priority sector did channel a significant amount of credit to agriculture and also led to a major expansion of the branch network of (public sector) banks in the rural areas. Nonetheless, a period of severe financial repression jeopardised the viability of many banks by the end of the 1980s. Profitability had declined from 23 per cent in 1975 all the way down to 9 per cent of total business (deposits plus credit) in 1984.

Although there were signs of the government's gradual loosening of the tight grip on commercial banks as early as in 1986, the banking sector reforms launched by RBI in 1991 based on the recommendations of the first Narasimham Committee on Financial Sector Reforms ended the era of rigid government control of banks and allowed entry of new private and foreign banks. Unlike in many other countries, these banking sector reforms were not triggered by any impending crisis. Nor were the reforms designed by any multi-lateral aid agency. Instead, they were indigenously formulated. Also, while market shares of domestic private and foreign banks were permitted to increase, there was no attempt to end government ownership by large-scale privatisation of existing public sector banks. Accommodation of new private domestic and foreign banks has lowered public sector banks' share in the total assets of the banking sector from 90 per cent in 1991 to less than 74 per cent in 2010. Even after nearly two decades since the reform was launched, public sector banks continue to dominate. Another interesting point needs to be noted. There was an initial phase of capital infusion into public sector banks by the government. Subsequently, their capital base was expanded by allowing private equity participation up to 49 per cent. Diversification of ownership diluted but did not eliminate their public sector character. At the same time, these banks now became accountable to shareholders and needed to improve efficiency.

While the first phase of financial reforms guided by the Report of the Narasimham Committee I (1991) was primarily designed to introduce "operational flexibility" and functional autonomy in order to improve productivity and efficiency of banks, the second phase, based on the subsequent Report of the Narasimham Committee II (1998), addressed the question of the banking sector's financial stability. Over the years of banking under rigid government control, the accumulating burden of non-performing loans (NPL) reached alarming proportions threatening many banks' solvency. To bring about financial stability, RBI adopted prudential banking norms consistent with the Basel Accord (1988) and the subsequent Basel II (2004). The three main components of these norms are (a) minimum capital requirement (enforced through statutory minimum capital to risk-weighted asset ratio (CRAR), (b) supervision and monitoring of risk management and (c) transparency in disclosure of specific variables that would enable financial markets to appropriately evaluate the bank. In India the mandatory capital adequacy ratio was set at 9 per cent, which exceeds the international norm of 8 per cent.

The reforms introduced significant changes in the Indian banking industry. The most important of all was increased competition introduced by more liberal rules for entry of new domestic and foreign banks. Initial infusion of government capital to rejuvenate public sector banks was followed by allowing private ownership of up to 49 per cent of total equity. In fact, up to 20 per cent of private equity can be held by foreign individuals and financial institutions. Foreign direct investment in private banks was now allowed up to 75 per cent. Interest rates on deposits and loans were deregulated. There was a reduction in statutory lending requirement and cash reserve requirements to ameliorate financial repression and reduce pre-emption of bank lending. Widening the coverage of "priority sector" offered greater flexibility to banks in respect of lending. International best practices and norms on risk-weighted capital adequacy requirements, accounting, income recognition, provisioning, and exposure were introduced and gradually implemented. To ensure creditors' rights, the Securitization and Reconstruction of Financial Assets and Enforcement of Securities Interest (SARFASEI) Act was promulgated and subsequently amended. A Credit Information Bureau for information sharing on defaulters and other borrowers was set up. The Board of Financial Supervision was set up as the apex supervisory authority for banks, financial institutions, and NBFCs. The so-called CAMELS supervisory rating system was introduced to introduce risk-based supervision. Greater transparency norms supplemented by market discipline aimed to enhance corporate governance.

Over the post-reform years, the share of NPL in total loans has declined dramatically. For example, the ratio of NPL to total advances declined from 15.7 per cent in 1996–97 to 2.4 per cent in 2009–10 for all scheduled commercial banks. For public sector banks, the corresponding decline was from 17.8 per cent in 1996–97 to 2.2 per cent in 2009–10.

Not surprisingly, the impact of banking reforms on Indian banks' performance has been researched extensively in numerous papers, which can be grouped into two broad categories: The first category comprises descriptive papers that compare popular measures of performance such as business per employee, intermediation cost per rupee of assets, credit-deposit ratio, or percentage of NPL in total credit over years and across ownership types of banks. Several papers by leading experts on Indian banking provide a comprehensive overview of banking reforms as an integral part of Financial Sector Reforms in India. Mohan (2004, 2005), Reddy (2005, 2008), and Rangarajan (2007) have described the motivation for and objectives of the reforms and have also looked into the initial experience of the Indian banking sector during the post-reform era. Particularly, Mohan (2004, 2005) highlighted the interrelationship between financial development and economic growth and assessed the impact of reforms on banks' efficiency and productivity using a number of alternative measures of performance such as business per employee, intermediation cost (as percentage of total assets), cost–income ratio, and net interest margin.

For the banking sector as a whole, there is clear evidence of decline in operating cost per unit of earning asset (often viewed as the unit cost of output). It fell from 2.08 per cent in 1992 almost steadily (except for a sudden increase in 1995 and 1996) to 1.78 per cent in 2004. As for intermediation cost (i.e. operating expense) as a percentage of earning assets, Indian private banks showed the maximum improvement, lowering it from 2.97 per cent in 1992 to 2.01 per cent in 2004. In fact, by this criterion, both public sector banks and private domestic banks were more efficient than foreign banks. But as Mohan (2004) cautioned, the lower intermediation cost must be weighed against the large expenditure incurred on upgrading the information technology and institution of "core banking". A different measure of performance is the cost–income ratio. For all scheduled commercial banks, the percentage of net income spent on operating cost declined from 55.3 per cent in 1992 to 45.1 per cent in 2004. Compared with domestic banks (both public and private), foreign banks had lower cost–income ratio. The share of net NPL (net of provisioning) in total advances also showed a decline from 8.1 per cent in 1996–97 to 1.8 per cent by 2002–03. As Mohan (2004) explained, there were several factors behind this decline. First, the high NPL accumulation in the banking sector was a legacy of poor credit decisions taken before reforms and were carried over from the past. Second, an improvement in credit appraisal has lowered the incremental accumulation of NPL even during a low growth phase of the economy in the late 1990s. Third, public sector banks have been more successful in loan recovery than the private domestic banks. Of course, foreign banks have had a better recovery ratio and lowest NPL ratio among all ownership groups. Overall, Mohan (2004, 2005) has provided ample evidence that reforms have brought about significant improvement in the performance of scheduled commercial banks in general and public sector banks in particular. Although highly informative and quite comprehensive in summarising changes between the pre- and post-reform decades, these papers are not grounded in any underlying conceptualisation of a production process in the banking industry.

In contrast, the papers in the second category of constitute the normative stand in the literature and use data to construct a production, cost, or profit function as a benchmark for comparison with the actual output, cost, or profit of a bank. Depending on the perceived objective of the bank, one would measure efficiency using output maximization, cost minimization, or profit maximization as criteria. In one of the early studies of the impact of the reforms, Bhattacharyya, et al. (1997) analysed the efficiency of public, private, and foreign banks using data from 1986–91. The time period is best described as the transition years of early deregulation before banking sector reforms were formally launched. They included deposit, credit, and investment as outputs. Interest expenses and operating expenses were treated as the two inputs. They found that public sector banks were the most efficient and private banks were the least efficient with foreign banks lying in between.

Covering a longer time period (1985–96), Kumbhakar and Sarkar (2003) estimated a Translog shadow cost function for public and private banks in India. They found that there was significant input price distortion due to regulation. This resulted in over-employment of labour relative to capital over the entire sample period in both public and private sector banks. This distortion declined gradually although somewhat faster

for private sector banks. Private banks experienced a higher rate of productivity growth than public sector banks. Also, their rate of productivity growth was higher during 1992–96 than during 1985–91. Ram Mohan and Ray (2004) used data for 1990–2000 to measure revenue maximization efficiency of the three categories of banks. Public sector banks were significantly more efficient than private banks in maximising revenue. There was no significant difference between public and foreign banks. Ram Mohan and Ray (2005) compared the rates of total factor productivity growth for the three ownership categories of banks during 1992–2000 measured by both the Tornqvist and the Malmquist productivity indexes. Public sector banks outperformed private sector banks but did worse than foreign banks if productivity growth is measured by the Malmquist index, but foreign banks do worse if one uses the Tornqvist index.

Das et al. (2005) examined the efficiency of Indian banks during 1997–2003 using revenue maximization and profit maximization as alternative objectives of banks. They treated loans, investments, and other income as the three outputs, labour, fixed assets, and borrowed funds as variable inputs, and equity as a quasi-fixed input. They found that different ownership groups did not differ much in respect of either technical efficiency or cost efficiency. However, there was sharp difference with respect to revenue efficiency and profit efficiency. An important finding of their study is that if a bank is listed in the Stock Exchange, it exhibits higher profit efficiency.

A bank's size was also found to positively influence profit efficiency. A more detailed analysis of the data covered in Das et al. (2009) was provided in Ray and Das (2009). Among public sector banks, SBI and its associates showed much higher profit efficiency than other nationalised banks. Foreign banks performed slightly worse than the SBI group but better than nationalised banks or domestic private banks. Regarding exposure to the Stock Exchange, listed banks operated at a much higher level of profit efficiency than non-listed banks. In 2003, the level of profit efficiency was 70.7 per cent for listed banks compared with 58.1 per cent for non-listed banks. Surprisingly, there was not much difference between the two categories regarding cost efficiency. A kernel density analysis of the distribution of profit efficiency in selected years shows that the entire distribution of profit efficiency of domestic banks has shifted outwards over years and that this was driven mainly by shift in public sector banks' profit efficiency distribution. Ketkar and Ketkar (2008) measured efficiency of banks in India for 1996–2003 using two alternative specifications of the production technology differing in their definition of inputs and outputs. Deposits are considered to be output in one version and input in another. They found that foreign banks were most efficient irrespective of whether deposits are considered output or input. Also, while efficiency has improved for all categories of banks, nationalised banks improved the most during the sample period.

To summarise the empirical evidence from the various studies reported here,[67] there is broad agreement that Indian banking reforms have improved the productivity of banks in all ownership categories. Many studies find that state-owned banks have operated at higher levels of efficiency than domestic private banks and usually above foreign banks as well. The findings are quite sensitive to the choice of inputs and outputs and also to the estimation methodology. Nevertheless, the broad empirical evidence does not agree with the popular belief, often held as axiomatic truth, that public sector firms governed by bureaucrats protected by attenuated accountability are less efficient than private firms, where managers are subject to a market discipline. Moreover, foreign firms with better management practices are expected to outperform domestic firms. How can one reconcile the empirical evidence with the prior expectation?

B. Empirical Analysis of Post-Reform Data

Productivity measurement in the service sector in general is quite difficult. Unlike in manufacturing, most outputs in the service sector are intangible and are only indirectly measureable. Often, service delivery requires the consumer's active participation (as in the case of physician's services). In many cases, output is produced on demand only and cannot be stored for future delivery. Finally, wide variation in quality makes quantitative measurement of output quite problematic. In case of banking, there is no universally accepted categorization of inputs and outputs, making things even more difficult. A typical commercial bank accepts deposits, makes commercial, real estate, and personal loans, makes investments in government securities as well as in private funds, and offers a variety of fee-based financial services. To carry out these activities, it utilises labour, physical capital, and IT capital.

While labour and capital are universally accepted as inputs and loans, investments, and other services are considered outputs, there is no consensus on whether

deposit is an input or an output. This ambiguity follows from two alternative views of the production process in the banking industry. In the so-called *production approach*, banks are viewed as service providers to the two broad categories of its customers: depositors and borrowers. Here, labour and capital are inputs and the numbers of deposit and credit transactions are the outputs. Given the lack of information on the numbers of *transactions,* numbers of the two kinds of *accounts* are used as measures of outputs. In contrast, in the *intermediation approach*, banks are seen to be intermediaries of funds from savers to investors. Banks collect funds by accepting deposits (and also by borrowing from lenders) and turn them into revenue-generating assets such as loans and investments. One version[68] of the *intermediation approach* is the *asset approach*, where the primary focus is on intermediation between depositors and final users of financial assets of the bank. In this approach, deposits along with labour and capital (both physical and IT) are considered inputs, while loans, investments, and financial services are treated as outputs. This *asset approach* is the most consistent with the characterization of a bank as a commercial enterprise that incurs costs on inputs to generate revenue from outputs.

Apart from deposits and borrowing, another potential source of funds for a bank is its own capital and reserves or *equity* that should also be counted as an input, especially in the asset approach. It should be noted, however, that compared with the other inputs, a bank has much less flexibility in altering the level of its equity, which is more like a quasi-fixed input in the short run. In the present study, deposits, fixed assets, labour, and equity (capital and reserves) are included as inputs and loans, investments, and other (non-interest) income are considered outputs. There is another problem with the measurement of efficiency in Indian banking, where banks of different ownership categories pursue different objectives. It is reasonable to assume that foreign and domestic banks in the private sector seek to maximise profit. For public sector banks, the objective is not so clear cut. Banks under government are legally required to pursue the government's social banking objectives. This requires them to direct 40 per cent of their total advances to the so-called priority sector and also invest a minimum required percentage in government securities. At the same time, these banks are expected to remain profitable to maintain their economic viability. Because efficiency measurement requires a comparison of the actual outcome with the optimal, the measured level of efficiency of a bank will be sensitive to the choice of a criterion function. One must bear in mind that there is no "one size fits all" objective function that applies to all banks while evaluating efficiency in Indian banking.

1. Descriptive Measures of Performance: Labour Productivity

Three most popular measures of productivity in banking are (a) total business (i.e. sum of deposit and credit) per employee, (b) credit-deposit ratio, and (c) intermediation cost. Out of these, business per employee appeals most to common sense because it is a measure of labour productivity when deposit and credit are considered to be the only two outputs. In this sense, it is grounded in the *production approach* described earlier.

Table 1 reports for selected years the annual averages of three descriptive indicators of performance. The figures reported are lakhs of rupees in constant 1993–94 prices. As expected, foreign banks outperform domestic banks by a large margin. Private domestic banks started below public sector banks but quickly caught up. In 1995, the two groups were at comparable levels. But the very next year there was a spectacular increase in business per employee at private banks. For public sector banks, the increase was quite marginal. During 1992–2000, on average private banks did better. However, by 2005 public sector banks made a significant gain and caught up to private banks in just one year. By 2008 they were clearly outperforming the private domestic banks al-

though over the sub-period 2001–09 private banks had a higher average. In general, all categories of banks improved in terms of business per employee. Foreign banks stayed above both types of domestic banks.

Simultaneously with business per employee, one should also look at the credit-deposit ratio. This gives an idea about the composition of "total business" narrowly defined as above. A bank may achieve the same level of business per employee by increasing deposits and reducing credit by the same amount. However, given that higher deposits entail additional interest expense while increased credit generates additional revenue for the bank, ranking bank productivity by business per employee is somewhat misleading even as a partial measure of productivity. Analysing the credit-deposit ratio is important for another reason. It is generally agreed that intermediation of funds from savers to investors is the most important contribution of the banking sector to the overall economic growth. Banerjee *et al.* (2004) have argued that Indian banks are under-lenders.

For the earlier sub-period (1991–2000), the credit-deposit ratio for the foreign banks was 0.59, much higher than those of the domestic banks, both public (0.48) and private (0.50). Some foreign banks had credit-deposit ratios exceeding 1 in selected years. Of course, a ratio greater than unity means that a bank has been lending out of its own (reserve) funds. But as noted by Ketkar and Ketkar (2007), many smaller foreign banks operating in India are virtual extensions of their own embassies and mainly service the nationals from those countries. Therefore, it may not be quite appropriate to compare credit-deposit ratios of domestic and foreign banks. Overall, however, it is evident that in post-reform years banks have increased credit relative to deposit. The third indicator of performance often used to compare banks is intermediation cost as a percentage of total assets. Conceptually, it is a somewhat distorted version of what is known as average cost in microeconomics text books. To be precise, average cost is measured by cost per unit of the output produced. If the total asset of a bank is used as proxy for its output and all non-interest expenses as the total cost, then intermediation cost as a fraction of its total assets is a crude measure of its average cost. Between 1992 and 2010, average intermediation cost for public sector banks has fallen from 2.6 per cent of total assets to below 1.5 per cent. Private domestic banks also show a downward trend, but the decline was far less pronounced than that ex-

Table 1.	Descriptive measures of performance		
Year	Public	Private	Foreign
Business per employee (Rs. lakh) averages			
1992–2000	57.86	156.87	530.60
2001–09	206.63	261.14	749.14
1992–2009	132.25	209.01	639.87
Credit-deposit ratio averages			
1992–2000	0.47	0.50	0.59
2001–09	0.58	0.57	0.62
1992–2009	0.53	0.53	0.61
Intermediation cost (% of assets)			
1993	2.64	2.71	2.7
2003	2.25	1.99	2.79
2010	1.49	1.97	2.56

perienced by the public sector banks. Surprisingly, foreign banks showed an initial increase followed by a downward movement in later years. Consistent with the much higher level of business per employee, the share of personnel cost in the total operating cost has been much lower for foreign banks. But computerization and much more widespread use of ATMs by foreign banks (and to some extent by the private banks) account for a greater share of non-labour expenses in total operating costs.

Given the asymmetric distribution of branches in rural and semi-urban areas, a substantially higher share of labour cost in total operating expenses of public sector banks is only to be expected. For example, in 2010 more than 55 per cent branches of public sector banks were located in rural and semi-urban areas, about 22 per cent in urban areas and less than 20 per cent in metropolitan cities. Private banks had 42 per cent of their branches in rural and semi-urban areas, 30 per cent in urban areas and 28 per cent in metropolitan cities. In contrast, 77 per cent of foreign bank branches were in metropolitan cities, 19 per cent in urban areas and a minimal presence in rural or semi-urban areas. This is reflected in the limited availability of ATMs for public sector banks. In 2010, there were 87 ATMs per 100 branches for public sector banks, 184 ATMs per 100 branches for private banks, and 10 ATMs for every 3 branches for foreign banks. Greater reliance on more sophisticated technology accounts for higher business per employee but greater intermediation cost for foreign banks.

An important development in the second phase of banking reforms that contributed significantly to a marked decline in the share of labour costs in the total operating expenses of public sector banks was the introduction of a voluntary retirement scheme (VRS) for employees in public sector banks in 2000. A Federation of Indian Chambers of Commerce and Industry (FICCI) report on the banking industry estimated that banks in India were overstaffed to the tune of about 35 per cent. The Finance Ministry estimated that even at the modest rate of Rs. 1 Crore of business per employee, there were 59,338 surplus employees in 12 nationalised banks. As banking reforms gathered momentum and government handouts tended to dry up, it became apparent that banks could no longer afford to carry excess manpower.

Workforce downsizing in highly unionised public sector banks was quite a challenge. After a long deliberation, in November 1999, the government introduced a voluntary severance package for public sector em-

ployees. Between November 2000 and March 2001, all public sector banks, except Corporation Bank, introduced a VRS. By March 2001, as many as 100,810 of the 863,117 employees of the 26 public sector banks accepted the offer. This 11 per cent reduction resulted in a dramatic reduction of labour cost within a year. However, there were problems of major disruption of services in the initial period because downsizing was implemented at once rather than in phases. Rational reallocation of employees across branches was time consuming. Also, many departing employees were more productive and senior workers, who were readily absorbed by new private sector banks. This explains (at least partially) why a marked reduction in the number of employees did not immediately translate into a jump in business per employee. But as the more recent evidence shows, things eventually ironed out and public sector banks emerged out of this process of adjustment successfully with a leaner and more productive work force.

2. Non-Performing Loans

An important objective of banking sector reforms, especially those recommended by the Narasimham Committee II, was to restore financial solvency of public sector banks by addressing the onerous burden of their accumulated non-performing loans and introducing prudential lending norms. Table 2 shows how the proportion of non-performing loans in the total advances of various categories of banks has declined over years. In this regard, it is useful to distinguish between "old" and "new" private banks. It may be recalled that by 1980 most of larger domestic banks were brought under direct government control through nationalization. The smaller ones that remained outside the public sector constituted the "old private" category. In contrast, the "new private" ones are the handful of banks established in the post-reform era. Ten new banks were formed in the private sector after the 1993 guidelines and two new banks after the 2001 revised guidelines. Only banks that had adequate experience in broad financial sector, financial resources, trustworthy people and strong and competent managerial support could withstand the rigorous demands of promoting and managing a bank. However, the "new" private banks had two advantages compared with public and "old private" banks: Starting from scratch, they could opt for modern banking technology at the outset, and unlike established banks, they did not carry the enormous burden of non-performing loans accumulated over years.

Table 2 shows markedly different time trends in the share of non-performing loans in total advances of different categories of banks. Back in 1992, nearly a quarter of the total loans made by public sector banks were in default. However, there was a steady decline in the share of non-performing loans over the years. By 2001, it came down to 12.4 per cent (half of what it was in 1992). It went further down to 5.5 per cent in 2005 and hovered around 2 per cent in 2009–10. By all accounts, it is a history of remarkable recovery to international standards (or better) from what was a precipitous risk of insolvency two decades earlier. Both the "new" private banks and foreign banks had a much lower proportion of non-performing loans. The "new" private banks performed better than foreign banks during 1997–2001 but somewhat worse thereafter. Overall, the public sector banks performed better than all categories of banks in respect of non-performing loans. It may be noted, in passing, that reduction in non-performing loans was achieved simultaneously with an increase in credit-deposit ratio. This suggests an improvement in the quality of loans instead of a reduction in the volume of loans (relative to deposits).

3. Labour Productivity and Efficiency

There are two main limitations of using a simple arithmetic measure such as business per employee as an indicator of productivity or efficiency. Even if we treat deposits as output and measure total output by the sum of deposits and credit, labour is not the only input in use. A lower share of employee costs in total intermediation costs implies a higher (physical) capital labour ratio for private and foreign banks. A bank with a higher number of ATMs will naturally be able to handle the same volume of business with fewer employees. The right question to ask is whether a bank produces the maximum amount of business with its existing number of employees and non-labour inputs. One way to answer the question is to focus on the *maximum amount of credit that can be offered* without changing any other output or input of the bank. The resulting level of business per employee is the right benchmark for comparison with the actual performance of a bank for evaluating its efficiency. To illustrate this point, the input-output data for individual banks[69] from 2009 were used to solve the DEA optimization problem where the objective was to maximise credit output without reducing any of the other two outputs (investment and fee-based income) and also without increasing any of the inputs (equity, deposits,

Table 2	Non-performing loans (per cent of total advances)			
Year	Public	Old private	New private	Foreign
1994	24.8	-	-	-
1995	19.5	-	-	-
1996	18	-	-	-
1997	17.8	10.7	2.6	4.3
1998	16	10.9	3.5	6.4
1999	15.9	13.1	6.2	7.6
2000	14	10.8	4.1	7
2001	12.4	10.9	5.1	6.8
2002	11.1	11	8.9	5.4
2003	9.4	8.9	6.7	5.3
2004	7.8	7.6	5	4.6
2005	5.5	6	3.6	2.8
...	...	...	...	...
2009	1.97	2.36	3.05	3.8
2010	2.19	2.32	2.87	4.29

fixed assets and labour). The optimal business per employee[70] was computed for each bank by replacing its actual credit by the maximum possible obtained from the DEA solutions. Obviously, its actual level of credit remains feasible for a bank in the optimization problem. Therefore, the optimal business per employee (BPE*) will not be any lower than the actual business per employee (BPE^0). The ratio of BPE^0 to the benchmark (BPE*) can be interpreted as one measure of the efficiency of a bank.

Of the top 15 of the 75 banks ranked in order of actual business per employee in 2009, all except IDBI Bank were foreign banks. But only 6 out of those 14 generated the maximum amount of business per employee that would be possible from their respective input bundles. Actual and maximum BPE for the selected

Table 3	Actual and optimal business per employee (Rs lakhs) 2009 data(for selected banks)		
Bank	bpe^0	bpe*	eff
Sonali Bank	54.13	54.13	1.00
United Bank of India	252.28	339.51	0.74
Allahabad Bank	298.35	402.13	0.74
Standard Chartered Bank	463.21	677.53	0.68
Abn Amro Bank	547.37	547.37	1.00
Bank of America	1389.18	1760.42	0.79

banks are reported in Table 3. Note that Allahabad Bank had higher BPE than United Bank of India, but both of them had the same level of efficiency in generating BPE. Bank of America had more than twice the BPE of ABN Amro Bank, but Bank of America was only 79 per cent efficient, whereas ABN Amro was fully efficient. At the lower end of spectrum, Sonali Bank was operating at full efficiency even though it had the lowest business per employee among the 75 banks. It should be emphasised that these examples are used only to show that a bank with a higher observed level of BPE need not be more efficient. The efficiencies reported in Table 3, being essentially one-dimensional in nature, are not intended to be interpreted as comprehensive measures of efficiency of these banks.

4. Overall Measures of Efficiency and Productivity Change: The Normative Analysis

A generalised or overall measure of efficiency should be computed against a benchmark that is Pareto efficient in the sense that there is no room for any net increase in output or a net decrease in input. One problem is that there are many bundles and all of them are Pareto efficient. For the present study, the benchmark selected for any individual bank is one that would lead to the maximum increase in TFP relative to the observed input-output bundle of the bank.

The data used for the empirical analysis is for 1992–2009 from an unbalanced panel of banks varying in number between 98 and 74 in different years. As already mentioned, SBI was excluded from the sample because of its extremely large size relative to all other banks. Also, several banks had to be excluded because of negative non-interest income in selected years. The summary statistics of the input-output data are reported for the three ownership categories in Table 4. All variables except labour are measured

in lakhs of Indian rupees at constant 1993–94 prices. Labour is measured by the number of persons employed. Table 6 shows that the average public sector bank is much bigger than private and foreign banks. This is true even if SBI is not included among the public sector banks. An average public sector bank is over 2.5 times larger than a private bank and more than 9.5 times larger than a foreign bank in terms of deposit or credit. Also, there is greater variability (judged by the coefficient of variation) among foreign and private banks than among the public sector banks.

Table 5 shows the group-wise average levels of Pareto–Koopmans efficiency and its two components – the input contraction factor and the output expansion factor. Averaged over all years and all banks in the sample, public sector banks are found to be the most efficient. Foreign banks come second and private banks come last. Over the different sub-periods reported in the table, public sector banks improved in efficiency from 0.946 to 0.963 before it experienced a slight decline to 0.944 during 2007–09. Foreign banks, on the other hand, started from a higher level of efficiency than public sector banks but became less efficient over the subsequent years. Private sector banks were less efficient to start with and became more so over later years. In this respect, the present study confirms the broad conclusion reached in the extant literature that on average public sector banks performed at a higher level of technical efficiency than both foreign banks and private domestic banks.

As explained above, technical inefficiency exists when there is room for increasing outputs without increasing inputs, or reducing inputs without reducing outputs, or some combination of both. Given the multiple input, multiple output nature of production in the banking industry, the potential for reduction in aggregate input can be measured by the weighted geometric mean

Table 4	Summary statistics		Equity	Deposits	Fixed assets	Labour	Credit	Investments	Other income
Public	Mean		107202.26	1704200.81	20469.99	23049.89	972507.86	646940.85	23477.60
	Std Dev		102539.62	1513798.28	22793.68	16422.78	1030719.61	497420.95	20999.38
Private	Mean		40151.77	449610.91	8814.59	3025.47	273768.94	172579.04	9147.98
	Std Dev		160675.35	1289268.22	26475.91	4710.51	904594.46	479126.71	32568.22
Foreign	Mean		26262.60	178570.39	4116.37	569.87	101913.86	69916.40	6565.79
	Std Dev		58595.70	384626.82	9651.49	1252.20	240621.12	145209.79	15665.32

Table 5	Overall efficiency and its decomposition (annual average)		
Year	**Public**	**Private**	**Foreign**
Pareto–Koopmans Efficiency			
1992–96	0.946	0.842	0.949
1997–2001	0.958	0.859	0.895
2002–06	0.963	0.841	0.885
2007–09	0.944	0.793	0.890
1992–2009	0.953	0.838	0.906
Input Contraction factor			
1992–96	0.963	0.945	0.961
1997–2001	0.961	0.913	0.936
2002–06	0.954	0.925	0.951
2007–09	0.932	0.898	0.951
1992–2009	0.955	0.923	0.949
Output Expansion factor			
1992–96	1.158	1.215	1.092
1997–2001	1.136	1.162	1.234
2002–06	1.101	1.160	1.511
2007–09	1.093	1.204	1.653
1992–2009	1.125	1.183	1.341

of the potential reduction in the individual inputs. This *input contraction factor* is a measure of the input-oriented technical efficiency of an individual bank. Similarly, the inverse of *output expansion factor* obtained in a parallel manner from potential increase in the individual outputs is the output-oriented efficiency. This factorization of the generalised Pareto–Koopmans efficiency provides a broad idea about the relative contribution of the two kinds of inefficiency – presence of surplus inputs and under achievement of potential outputs – to overall inefficiency.

Regarding input efficiency, for any of the three ownership types, there is little room for economising on the use of inputs. Public sector and foreign banks are about at par. Private sector banks show a slightly lower (but still high) level of input efficiency. The 2007–09 sub-period is the only time when any one of the three types (namely the private domestic banks) show input inefficiency of over 10 per cent. In contrast, as revealed by the output expansion factor, there was room to increase output by 12.5 per cent in the public sector banks, by 18.3 per cent in private domestic banks and by 34.1 per cent in foreign banks. Also, while

public sector banks improved in output efficiency over the sub-periods, foreign banks became worse. In fact, because of this large output inefficiency, foreign banks are less efficient than public sector banks. Further disaggregation shown in Table 6 identifies the total inefficiency that comes from each individual input and output. The column marked "Foreign" shows the average values of the input contraction and output expansion factors when all of the foreign banks in the sample are included. The entry in this column for Loans (φ_1) implies that on average foreign banks would be able to lend eight times as much as they are doing now without reducing any output or decreasing any input. This unrealistic figure is the result of including three individual banks (KBC Bank, Krung Thai Bank, and Oman International Bank) that reported abnormally low credit amounts in selected years. The recomputed averages for the foreign banks excluding these three are reported in column "Foreign*". Now the expansion factor for Loans comes down from 8.15 to 2.104, which, although much higher, is still in line with what we get for the other groups of banks. This would lower the overall output expansion factor for foreign banks from 1.34 to 1.29.

This output expansion factor explains, at least in part, why foreign banks are less efficient than public sector banks. Their output expansion factor of 2.01 for loans (φ_1) implies that foreign banks should lend twice as much as they are actually doing. This target is based on the assumption that all banks in the sample face the same kind of markets. To the extent that regulations limit the kind of loans that a foreign bank is permitted to make, this assumption becomes invalid. If a low volume of loans made by foreign banks is the result of inadequate or restricted demand, it should not necessarily be construed to be a sign of their inefficiency. This is a speculative rather than conclusive explanation of lower efficiency of foreign banks.

Table 6	Specific input/output efficiency factors			
		Public	**Private**	**Foreign**	**Foreign***
Deposits	$\theta 1$	0.983	0.986	0.994	0.994
Labour	$\theta 2$	0.801	0.666	0.771	0.781
Capital	$\theta 3$	0.774	0.720	0.862	0.862
Loans	φ^1	1.071	1.085	8.185	2.01
Investment	φ^2	1.051	1.136	1.199	1.191
Others	φ^3	1.870	2.334	2.104	1.901

Given the special interest focussed on labour productivity, the year-wise average of the input contraction factor for labour is reported for the different groups of banks separately in Table 7. The average over the entire data period (1992–2009) shows that foreign banks can cut down employment by 13.6 per cent. The comparable figures for public and private banks are 22.6 and 28.6 per cent, respectively. The percentage of surplus labour was much higher during the initial years for all domestic banks – both public and private. But the voluntary retirement scheme introduced in 2000 seems to have improved labour use efficiency in public sector banks. Their labour use efficiency jumped from 0.772 in 1997–2001 to 0.887 during 2002–06. Despite a slight deterioration, they were at the same level as foreign banks during 2007–09. During this last sub-period, private domestic banks fared much worse in this respect. While this may come as a shock to many people, the evidence is that public sector banks do not have any more surplus labour than foreign banks do!

Table 7			
Year	**Public**	**Private**	**Foreign**
1992–96	0.614	0.614	0.893
1997–2001	0.772	0.723	0.857
2002–06	0.887	0.836	0.847
2007–09	0.855	0.663	0.860
1992–09	0.774	0.714	0.865

Table 8 shows, respectively, the annual average rates of TFPG, technical efficiency change, and scale efficiency change for the different ownership groups of banks for selected years. Over the entire sample period, foreign banks experienced productivity growth at an annual rate of 3 per cent. Private banks came next with 0.5 per cent. Public sector banks were the slowest in productivity growth with 0.1 per cent annual rate. There are two main reasons for this lower rate of TFPG for public banks. First, public sector banks had higher total factor productivity than private or foreign banks. Therefore, in a relative sense, there was less room for improvement. Second, the data do not include SBI, the most important bank in this group.

All bank groups improved in respect of both technical efficiency and scale efficiency. As a group, foreign banks experienced an improvement in technical efficiency at the rate of 2.9 per cent per year over the sample period. By comparison, domestic private banks improved at a slower rate of 0.6 per cent annually

Table 8	Components of TFP growth rate (annual average)		
Year	**Public**	**Private**	**Foreign**
TFP growth			
1992–96	-0.031	-0.015	0.003
1997–2001	0.021	0.029	0.062
2002–06	-0.012	-0.007	0.001
2007–09	0.001	-0.010	0.021
1992–2009	0.001	0.005	0.030
Technical Efficiency Change			
1992–96	0.012	0.025	0.000
1997–2001	-0.004	0.913	0.936
2002–06	0.000	0.000	0.006
2007–09	0.006	0.000	0.102
1992–2009	0.003	0.006	0.029
Scale efficiency change			
1992–96	-0.042	-0.035	0.010
1997–2001	0.936	0.936	0.936
2002–06	0.009	0.007	0.025
2007–09	-0.004	-0.009	-0.015
1992–2009	0.005	0.001	0.022

nually and public sector banks at an even slower rate of only 0.3 per cent. In a multiple-input, multiple-output case, an intuitive interpretation of scale efficiency is rather difficult. In a broad sense, the numbers reported in Table 8 show that the technically efficient projections of all categories of banks moved closer to their most projections over time. However, these figures hide a puzzle about the implied rate of technical change.

Changes in total factor productivity are caused by changes in technical and scale efficiencies, on the one hand, and technical change (reflected by shifts in the frontier), on the other. The non-parametric method used in this study allows the frontier to shift at different rates at different data points. Also, both outward shift (implying technical progress) and inward shifts (implying technical regress) are allowed. A numerical measure of the rate of technical change can be obtained from the difference between the rate of TFP change and the sum of the rates of change in technical and scale efficiencies. By this measure, all three types of banks experienced *technical regress*. The rates of technical regress were 2.1 per cent per year in case of foreign banks, 0.6 per cent for public sector banks and 0.2 per cent for private domestic banks. Technological retrogression implies an inward shift of the frontier following the reforms. However, that would, indeed, repudiate all the claims made so far about the beneficial impact of Liberalization. However, a simple explanation of this puzzle is possible. In banking, where production consists primarily of converting loanable funds into advances and other revenue-generating assets, the frontier can move in or out due to changes in the overall economic conditions of the country in different years. Therefore, although computerization and installation of ATMs do push the frontier outwards, demand fluctuations related to macroeconomic factors can push the frontier backwards. One must be careful about interpreting the negative residual change as technical regress.

C. Does Foreign Ownership of Equity Matter?

As stated at the very outset, India's banking reforms are nested within an overall package of economy-wide measures of Liberalization and globalization. An important component of Liberalization is relaxation of entry restrictions against foreign investment along with the promotion of the private sector within. Consistent with this pattern, apart from allowing entry by new private banks, the reforms also permit private equity holding of up to 49 per cent in public sector banks. Moreover, up to 20 per cent of this private eq-

uity can be held by foreign investors – individual or institutional. In case of private domestic banks, foreign direct investment up to 75 per cent of total equity is permitted. It is generally believed that foreign equity participation enhances productivity by introducing international standards of professionalism in management. The greater the share of foreign equity in a bank, the more likely is it to benefit from such influences. Hence, a greater share of foreign equity can be expected to improve productivity. At the same time, from the empirical evidence in the literature, it appears that government ownership (possibly due to economies of scale enjoyed by the public sector banks) has a positive impact on productivity and efficiency.

To statistically test the effect of foreign equity holding on bank efficiency, the 2009 efficiency scores of 47 domestic banks were regressed on an ownership variable, PUBLIC, and another variable measuring foreign equity share (FOREIGN_SHARE). The ownership dummy variable assumed value 1 for public sector banks and 0 for private domestic banks. Of the 47 domestic banks in the sample, 26 were in the public sector. SBI was excluded from the sample. There was considerable variation in foreign equity ownership both among private and public banks. Among public sector banks, Punjab National Bank, with 19.1 per cent foreign ownership, was close to the statutory upper limit of 20 per cent. Union Bank of India (17.5 per

Table 9	Regression of 2009 efficiency of domestic banks				
Model 1					
Dependent: Eff2009					
Independent		Coefficient	std. err.	t-ratio	p-value
Constant		0.6726	0.0419	16.03	<0.0001
PUBLIC		0.2405	0.0416	5.78	<0.0001
FOREIGN_SHARE		0.0033	0.001	3.12	0.0032
R^2	0.4338	$N = 47$			
$\overline{R}^2$	0.4081				
Model 2					
Dependent: Eff2009					
		Coefficient	std. err.	t-ratio	p-value
Constant		0.709	0.0495	14.3116	0
PUBLIC		0.2059	0.0553	3.7227	0.0004
FOREIGN_SHARE		0.0014	0.0006	2.2528	0.0274
CONPLAINTS_ACCOUNTS		0.0004	0.0003	1.3954	0.1673
COMPLAINTS_CARDS		0.002	0.0012	1.6052	0.113
R^2	0.232	N -75			
$\overline{R}^2$	0.188				

cent) and Bank of Baroda (17.1 per cent) were also quite close. At the same time, there were public sector banks with no foreign equity. Among banks in the private sector, IndusInd Bank (68.5 per cent). ING Vaisya Bank (67.3 per cent) and ICICI Bank (66.3 per cent) had the highest percentages of foreign ownership. Only a handful of private banks had no or nominal foreign equity. Table 9 shows the estimated regression model. All the coefficients were statistically significant. The ownership dummy was positive highly significant showing that the expected efficiency of a bank with no foreign equity would increase from 0.672 if it was in the private sector to 0.912 if it was a public bank. This was expected, but the more important finding was that for any ownership type, a domestic bank's efficiency increases by 0.003 with 1 per cent increase in foreign equity share. The R^2 of the model is a reasonable 0.43 suggesting that the model is adequate. Although based on a single-year cross section data, this regression provides empirical evidence favouring the hypothesis that foreign equity participation has helped improve efficiency in Indian banking.

D. Productivity and Service Quality

An important aspect of productivity that is generally ignored in the banking literature is the quality of service provided to customers. While quality is an important dimension of output in every industry, it is much more so in banking, where every transaction between a customer and an employee is unique and variation in quality can be enormous. Often a greater volume of transactions is accomplished at the expense of the personal service that a customer at the counter deserves. While variability in quality is acknowledged, researchers typically have to rely on customer satisfaction surveys, which are quite expensive, not always accurate and often poorly designed. There is a popular belief that foreign banks offer a better quality of customer service than bureaucratically run public sector banks or even private domestic banks. Because providing better quality of service consumes resources (in terms of employee time), one can expect a lower volume of output if a higher standard of quality is to be maintained. A logical implication of this quality-quantity trade-off is that a bank can improve productivity by lowering quality. It is interesting to empirically investigate whether a higher level of measured efficiency of a bank has, in fact, been attained by providing a poorer quality of service.

It is possible to measure quality of service by the number of customer complaints against a bank registered with the Banking Ombudsman office. Customer complaints can be divided into two categories: (i) related to deposit or credit accounts and (ii) related to credit or debit cards. Account-related complaints typically involve services offered at a branch. By contrast, card-related complaints pertain mostly to electronic fund transfers. Two variables, COMPLAINTS_ACCOUNT and COMPLAINTS_CARDS are used to measure levels of consumer dissatisfaction with these two types of services. Based on the data obtained from Report on Trend and Progress of Banking in India 2009–10,[71] the average numbers of complaints per 100,000 accounts during the year 2009–10 were 6 for public sector banks, 18 for private banks, and 51 for foreign banks. Within the category of private banks, the average numbers were 4 for old private banks and 25 for new private banks. During the same period, the average numbers (per 100,000 accounts) of card-related complaints were 7 for public sector banks, 8 for private banks, and 40 for foreign banks. Although these numbers are based on one-year data, they challenge the notion of superior quality of service provided by foreign banks.

To measure the impact to lower quality on the efficiency score of a bank, an extended regression including these two complaint variables was estimated using the 2009 data. For this regression all 75 observations (including the 28 foreign banks for that year) were used. By definition, foreign equity share was set at 100 per cent for all foreign banks. The results are shown in the lower part of Table 9. Estimated coefficients of both complaint variables were positive although not significant at the usual 5 per cent or 10 per cent levels. The coefficient of the account-related complaints variable has p-value of 0.167 while the other had a p-value of 0.113. The coefficients of the other variables, the ownership dummy and foreign equity share retained from the previous regression remain highly significant although they are both attenuated in size. The R^2 on the model was 0.232. Given that it includes both domestic and foreign banks, a greater heterogeneity in the data accounts for this lower goodness of fit. An interesting application of this model would be to compare quality-adjusted efficiency across the bank groups. If private and foreign banks had the same rate of complaints as public sector banks in 2009, the predicted average efficiency would be 0.9396 for public banks, 0.7563 for private domestic banks and 0.8124 for foreign banks. This shows that once adjusted for quality, the difference in efficiency between public and foreign banks in 2009 was greater than what the unadjusted measures suggest.

E. Direct Comparison of Total Factor Productivity: A Tale of Three Banks

All of the results comparing public, private, and foreign banks along different coordinates of performance are reported in terms of group- and year-wise averages in the various tables. An important limitation of comparing groups in terms of averages is that there can be considerable variation within the groups around the respective group means. This is particularly true for foreign and domestic banks, where outstanding banks coexist with very weak banks.In a sense, it is much more informative to directly compare the best banks from the different categories one on one. This also matches the popular approach where the best private bank is pitted against the best public or foreign bank. One can select ICICI Bank among the private banks and HSBC among foreign banks as the iconic banks of their respective categories. Among public sector banks, the automatic choice would be SBI. We cannot compare the efficiency levels of these banks directly because SBI was excluded from the normative analysis. However, it is possible to compute descriptive measures of total factor productivity index from the weighted quantity ratios of individual outputs and individual inputs of any pair of banks. This total factor productivity index also shows the ratio of the overall levels of technical efficiency of these to banks.

For this comparison, the input-output bundle of SBI in 1992 was treated as the reference bundle and the input-output quantities of all of the three banks – ICICI Bank, HSBC, and SBI itself – for 1996–2009 were used to compute total factor productivity index for these years. An advantage of using this index (which actually is a Tornqvist productivity index) is its multilateral applicability. For any bank, comparison across years reflects how its TFP has moved over time. In any year, comparison across banks shows how their TFP compare at a given point in time. In creating the index, the weights assigned were 0.71 for deposits, 0.19 to labour and 0.10 to fixed assets (i.e. physical capital). Among outputs, loans and investments were given 43 per cent weight each, while fee-based income was assigned 14 per cent weight. Because the monetary values were all deflated by the wholesale price index (1993–94 as the base), the deflated values were treated as quantities.

The TFP for individual banks reported in Table 10 clearly reveal the superior productivity levels of both ICICI Bank and HSBC relative to SBI. ICICI Bank emerges as the best performing bank, clearly dominating SBI in every year during 1997–2009. It also outperformed HSBC in most years. On the few occasions when it performed at a lower level than HSBC, the difference was quite small. HSBC had a lower productivity than SBI only in 1997 but thereafter was well ahead in terms of TFP. Looking at SBI's record over time, there is evidence of productivity decline during earlier years, but in 2000 there was a turnaround although productivity still remained below the level reached in 1992. Starting from 2001, TFP at SBI took an upward trajectory and continued to grow more or less steadily over the remaining years of the sample. This simple analysis shows that the best among the private and foreign banks were more productive than the best public bank. In this sense, the popular perception is ultimately vindicated. But this does not show that foreign or private banks *in general* are more efficient than public sector banks.

Table 10	Direct comparison of productivity change of three major banks		
Year	SBI	HSBC	ICICI
1996	1.025	0.988	1.288
1997	0.971	1.033	1.078
1998	0.967	1.052	1.081
1999	0.929	1.026	1.15
2000	0.998	1.136	1.24
2001	1.059	1.279	1.125
2002	1.103	1.261	1.3
2003	1.224	1.495	1.58
2004	1.288	1.584	1.55
2005	1.296	1.571	1.499
2006	1.277	1.569	1.511
2007	1.224	1.393	1.529
2008	1.284	1.496	1.612
2009	1.379	1.692	1.652

Note: Base: SBI 1992 = 1.

The main findings from this chapter can be summarised as follows:

- There has been a general increase in total factor productivity of all categories of banks – public, private, and foreign. Productivity growth was higher among foreign banks than domestic banks.

- Improvement in technical efficiency was a main factor behind productivity growth.
- As a group, public sector banks were more efficient than foreign banks. This was evident despite the fact that SBI, the iconic bank in that category, was excluded from the analysis. Private domestic banks were substantially less efficient than foreign banks.
- In a direct comparison of the three leading banks from the different ownership groups, ICICI Bank from the private domestic category had the highest total factor productivity. HSBC, a major foreign bank, came a close second, while SBI was a distant third.
- The government's effort to downsize employment in public sector banks through the voluntary retirement scheme launched in 2000 seems to have paid off in the form of improved total factor productivity down the road.
- A higher share of foreign ownership of equity has a beneficial impact on a bank's efficiency. This is true for both private and public sector banks.
- Higher productivity on standard input-output measures of a bank may hide quality-quantity trade-off. When adjusted for quality (based on the average number of customer complaints registered with the Banking Ombudsman Office), foreign banks' efficiency would be much lower than what was otherwise found for 2009. This is in conflict with the popular perception that foreign banks offer a higher quality of customer service.

F. Lessons from India's Experience

Given the increasingly important role India is poised to assume as an emerging giant in the global economic landscape, academics and policymakers have considerable interest in what other developing economies can learn from India's economic reforms in general and banking sector reforms in particular. The outcome of every social experiment contains both universal features that can be carried over to other situations and specific features that are unique to the context where the experiment was actually carried out. India's banking reforms were not prompted by a crisis. Nor were the broad contours of the reforms dictated by any agency providing multi-lateral aid. It was a deliberate and gradualist attempt to allow a greater role for private and foreign banks to improve efficiency through

competition. There was no all-out privatisation of public sector banks. However, allowing limited private ownership of government banks made them accountable to shareholders and subject to the market discipline. Going a step beyond partial privatisation, the reforms permitted limited foreign equity participation in domestic banks. By 2009, even at SBI, arguably the poster child of public sector banking, 13.8 per cent of its equity was held by foreign investors (institution and individual). This, by all accounts, is a far cry from the heyday of total government control of banks when employees in a typical branch of a public sector bank acted like a direct government official and treated its customers with the same kind of bureaucratic contempt.

While much of the criticism heaped on India's dysfunctional public sector banks is well deserved, it is seldom recognised that one of the objectives of nationalization of the major private banks was to use them as agents of social change. Much is said about financial repression and pre-emption of funds enforced through cash reserve requirement and statutory lending requirement. It is seldom recalled that one factor that prompted bank nationalization (especially in 1969) and directed credit requirement was the monopsonistic control on bank credit enjoyed by major industrial houses that diverted the flow of funds away from projects with high social benefit. India's social banking objective required these public sector banks to create a vast network of rural branches that were seldom economically profitable. There was an inherent conflict between the objectives of commercial profitability, on one the hand, and financial inclusion and universal banking on the other. In light of this, one would naturally make concessions for the non-commercial goals while evaluating the performance of public sector banks in terms of the standard financial ratio measures. However, lack of accountability coupled with job security over years turned these banks into non-performing juggernauts. Well protected by militant labour unions, bank employees (especially those in clerical positions) could engage in shirking and featherbedding with impunity.

By making room for competition from domestic and foreign banks, the Liberalization measures served as a virtual wake-up call to complacent public sector banks forcing them to regain economic viability through higher productivity and also to retain business by becoming more sensitive to customer needs. Trimming the workforce through severance incentives proved to be an effective way to improve productivity. Also after an initial infusion of capital into banks that were struggling to survive, the government refused to continue providing life support. Instead, banks were sent to the capital market to raise equity. This, naturally, had a sobering effect on top level management, who recognised that their performance would henceforth be under close market scrutiny. There is ample evidence in the published research that banks which are listed in the market were more profit efficient than those that were not.

An important feature of the Indian approach was that the social banking objectives were not discarded to make room for privatisation. Instead of discontinuing the requirement of priority sector lending, the government widened the coverage of the priority sector giving banks a wider choice in meeting their directed credit obligations. Similarly, a lowering of the statutory lending requirement forced the government to rely more on the securities market to raise the required funds at market-determined interest rates. This also released funds for banks to allocate to assets generating higher revenue. The two major objectives of banking reforms were to secure operational efficiency and to ensure financial solvency. The accumulated burden of non-performing loans pushed many public sector banks to the brink of financial insolvency. New prudential norms consistent with the Basel Accord brought the risk-quality of loans into prominence and a risk-weighted capital adequacy ratio set at 9 per cent (which is higher than the international norm) signalled the government's priority given to banks' financial soundness. Legislative changes were also introduced to secure creditor's rights and to facilitate recovery of bad loans.

While banks of all categories have succeeded in bringing down the proportion of non-performing loans in their total advances, the record is especially remarkable for public sector banks.

It needs to be emphasised that Liberalization did not allow private banks a free hand by any means. As stated by Mohan (2004), ownership and governance in private banks is a matter of great importance to the whole population because the owners or shareholders of the banks have only a minor stake and are in a position to leverage an enormous volume of other people's funds with little risk of personal loss. This grim warning pronounced in 2004 sounds almost prophetic in the aftermath of the global financial crisis. The fact that unscrupulous bankers and hedge fund managers in the United States and major European countries, where banks are under private ownership, were able to unleash this disaster should give pause to champions of unregulated banking. The new guidelines for private banks are designed to ensure competence, prudence, and transparency. Every country needs to design a structure of its banking industry that fits well with its own overall development strategy. India's dominant public sector within the banking industry is a legacy of a statist development policy that relied on direct public investment for infrastructure and rural development projects that fell below the radar of a profit-maximising private sector. India's banking sector reforms constitute an effort to strike a proper balance between the social banking goals, on the one hand, and cost-efficient intermediation of funds from savers to investors, on the other.

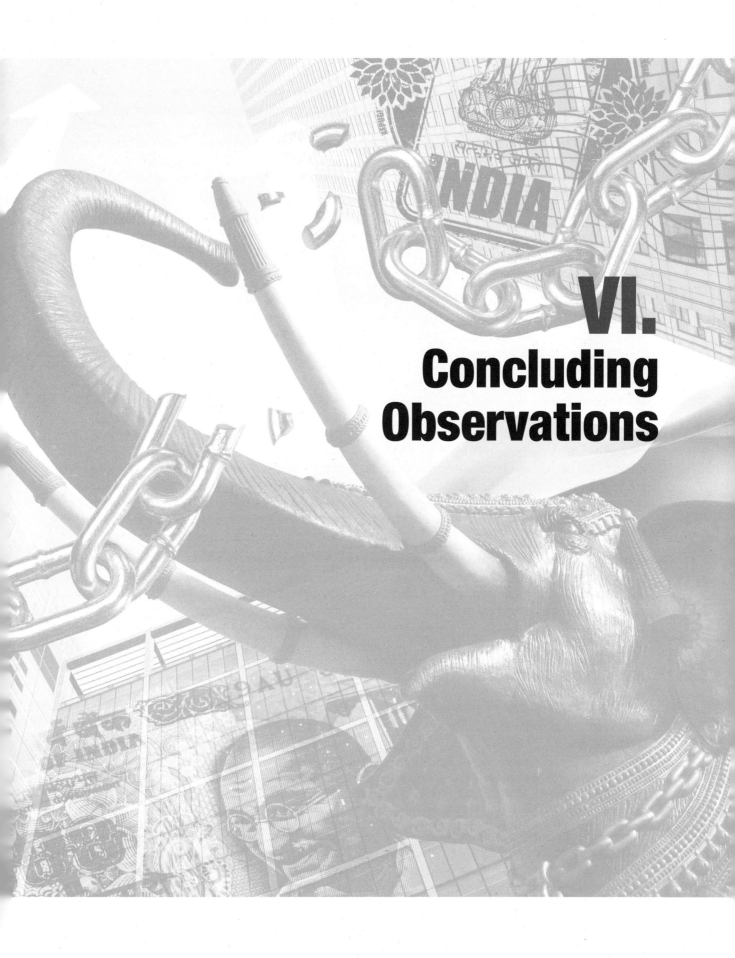

VI.
Concluding Observations

The global economic crisis in 2008 has fuelled debates on the link between Liberalization and growth. Conventional theories of export-led growth are being challenged, and growing financial Liberalization is being viewed with concern. This has drawn attention to the experiences of some developing countries, such as India, that have enjoyed a sustained period of strong economic growth, over a decade or more, to become 'emerging economies'. This book attempts to document India's experiences of twenty years of Liberalization and record the lessons learnt from its growth process.

One of the most striking features of India's Liberalization has been the slow and calibrated financial Liberalization, against the fast-pace and broad-based one in many other developing countries. Financial Liberalization in India was not considered an end in itself but the process to facilitate and encourage competitive business environment without risking too much coupling with the global financial markets. According to Ray and Virmani, the reforms of 1990s improved allocation of funds to reap the benefits of static welfare efficiency but did not aim to increase competitive supply of funds to new entrepreneurs, credit-rationed producers and (direct) investors. Further, opening up of the financial sector to foreign players was also gradual and is still limited.

India's financial Liberalization can be characterised as a cautious sequencing of mutually reinforcing norms and reforms. Some of the noteworthy reforms were prudential regulations comprising increase in capital adequacy ratio, risk weights to various securities and a review of functions of bank boards. It also included deregulation of interest rates, strengthening of institutional mechanism for monitoring and oversight, relaxing restrictions on foreign banks' ownership conditions and gradual increase in FDI limits in the banking sector. Statutory liquidity ratio (SLR) emerged as a genuine prudential tool ensuring the safety of the banking system. In addition, a number of legal and institutional measures were undertaken, including the settling up of Lok Adalats (people's courts), debt recovery tribunals and asset reconstruction companies.

The reforms resulted in marked improvement in the quality of banks' balance sheets. Over the last decade, Ray and Virmani estimate, the gross non-performing assets (NPAs) as a percentage of total gross advances of the banking sector came down from nearly 15 per cent to less than 3 per cent and net NPAs reduced from more than 7 per cent to around 1 per cent. Fur-

ther, the Indian corporate sector has been able to raise funds through a variety of resources. In 2009–10, nearly 55 percent of the total flow of resources came from non-banks and more than 20 per cent from foreign resources. Thus, the popular description of the Indian financial system as a closed bank-based system changed with the introduction of reforms.

The transformation in the foreign exchange management policy began with the introduction of partial convertibility of the rupee in 1992. The rupee–foreign currency swap was allowed and additional hedging instruments such as foreign currency–rupee options, cross-currency options, interest rate swaps (IRS) and currency swaps, caps/ collars and forward rate agreements (FRAs) were introduced. Another significant reform was the move towards corporatization and demutualization of stock exchanges and opening up of the mutual funds industry, which was earlier the monopoly of the public sector, to the private sector in 1992. The stock market over the last two decades has shown considerable buoyancy in its activity levels and National Stock Exchange of India has been ranked worldwide fifth in terms of turnover in the derivative market in 2011. While the capital account has been liberalised in a calibrated manner, India has clearly recognised a hierarchy in capital flows and has favoured equity flows over debt flows and foreign direct investment (FDI) over portfolio investments.

Has capital account Liberalization in India served the country well? According to Ray and Virmani, the lesson from the global financial crisis is perhaps better to be measured and safe rather than fast and rash. Financial Liberalization in India improved the allocation of funds and allowed the economy to grow, but given the fiscal deficit and inflation configuration, the opening up of the financial sector to foreign players has been calibrated. An important lesson learnt is that the calibrated pace of reforms and no policy reversals have ensured safety and stability to the financial system. Indian experience shows that the policymaker can devise intermediate outcomes instead of corner solutions.

However, India has been more experimental in the manufacturing sector, especially because industrial growth eluded India for a long time. From import substitution policies of the 1950s to export promotion strategies of 1980s to major tariff Liberalization of the 1990s, the sector has remained the focus of reforms. In spite of these efforts, it has been observed that till late 1990s, protection to the sector remained high. Also, the sector's average annual growth rate remained sticky at 5 to 6 per cent and its contribution to GDP remained less than 15 per cent with negligible growth in its employment. The 2000s witnessed a careful lowering of protection along with other complementary reforms. Reduction in weighted average of tariffs from 24 per cent in 2001 to 7 per cent in 2009 and, more important, removal of quantitative restrictions (QRs) for most of the items in 2001 were accompanied by important steps to boost exports. Changes were brought in the policy of reserving production of certain items for the small-scale sector. Some exportable products were removed from the reserved list in early 2000.

Banga and Das estimate the impact of reforms in this sector on its growth and conclude that in early 2000s, there was a structural break in the growth of real exports and real imports along with a structural shift in the growth of the organised manufacturing sector. This clearly indicates that tariff Liberalization and export promotion played an important role in pushing manufacturing growth from 5 per cent in previous decades to 8 per cent in the 2000s. Nevertheless, the role of domestic demand in the growth of this sector cannot be ignored, since during this period, India's per capita income grew, for the first time, at above 5 per cent annual average. The authors conclude that the causality ran from strong domestic demand and import Liberalization ® output growth ® export growth. Indian manufacturing growth is therefore not found to be an export-led growth although exports grew at an average rate of 10 per cent in this decade. This could also be a plausible reason for high resilience of India's growth to global slowdown as external demand played a limited role in its growth process. Import Liberalization, on the other hand, played a much more significant role. Tariff Liberalization has been faster for capital goods and industrial supplies compared with consumer goods. It was only in the 2000s that tariffs for consumer durables fell. Higher imports of technology via capital goods and better quality inputs increased productivity, efficiency and competitiveness of the sector, and the sector was able to face import competition, which was introduced much later. Sequencing of Liberalization in a phased manner seems to have leveraged the positive impacts of inducing domestic competition. This is an important lesson from India's Liberalization experience with respect to its manufacturing sector.

Another important finding is that in some industries such as electrical machinery and apparatus, chemicals and chemical products, and machinery and equipment, the import content of manufacturing exports is rising. These industries have experienced decline in value added growth but a rise in export and import growth during the 2000s compared with the 1990s. Many policy incentives were given to these industries to facilitate their imports of inputs. However, the more these export-oriented industries link to the global supply chains, the more they delink from domestic production networks. This is a concern for the economy as the potential advantages of a robust export growth spills to the external sector and can lead to potential dangers of "hollowing out".

The importance of the Indian agriculture sector cannot be understated. This sector not only provides food security for the country but also provides livelihood to more than 50 per cent of the population and hosts maximum number of people under disguised unemployment. It is therefore not surprising that since independence India has followed an inward looking and highly protectionist trade policy for this sector. Barring a few traditional commercial commodities, agricultural trade has been subjected to measures such as QRs, canalization, licenses, quotas and high tariff rates to regulate the sector's imports and exports in order to safeguard interest of domestic producers and domestic consumers. However, this scenario changed slowly with the initiation of economic reforms of 1991, and external trade was further liberalised with the implementation of the WTO Agreement on Agriculture in 1995. The process was accelerated after India lost the dispute in WTO to retain QRs on grounds of balance of payments.

This sector witnessed some efforts of Liberalization in the 2000s. Average tariffs for agriculture declined from around 49 per cent in the 1990s to 37 per cent in the 2000s. Nevertheless, it is interesting that tariffs increased for many important agricultural products, including rice, wheat, maize, sugar, tea, coffee and milk, in the 2000s. This was probably a response to the removal of QRs. The only agricultural item for which real Liberalization of import has taken place is vegetable oil: Even very high level of import duty could not check its import. In all other cases, imports are encouraged only when domestic supply cannot match domestic demand, e.g. pulses, and when there are temporary supply shocks like in the case of cotton and sugar and earlier even in the case of wheat. Realising the economy's potential to export agricultural products, various restrictions and controls on exports have been gradually removed and some indirect incentives have been put in place.

Chand and Bajar observe that India has followed a considerably flexible trade policy in agriculture, which has responded quickly to the changing global conditions. The guiding principle for opening up has been to allow domestic prices to move in tandem with the trend in global prices but insulate against sharp spikes and troughs. For instance, significant changes were made in export and import Liberalization policies after 2006–07, when global prices started increasing with the onset of the global food crisis. Between 2003–04 and 2008–09, global food prices increased by 83 per cent and ratio of agriculture exports to output increased by 62 per cent. Nevertheless, to protect domestic consumers, export restrictions were placed on main staples such as rice and wheat. During 2007–11, agricultural trade was strictly regulated by various notifications by the Directorate General of Foreign Trade. For example, to discourage the export of skimmed milk products, duty concession on their export was withdrawn in January 2011. Another significant change in trade policy during the 2000s was the steep reduction in import duty on vegetable oils, which constituted more than one third of India's agriculture food import. From 1991 to 2010, India's agriculture exports increased from $3 billion to $20 billion while agricultural imports increased 13 times, from $0.67 billion to $13 billion. India continues to enjoy trade surplus in agriculture.

An important lesson from India's experience in its trade policy for agriculture, according to Chand and Bajar, is that market forces cannot safeguard against global shocks such as food crisis and financial crisis. Therefore, government regulation and intervention are essential to safeguard domestic economies and vulnerable population. With active government intervention in 2007 and 2008, when the world faced the food crisis, India protected its market effectively and managed its food situation comfortably. Year on year, inflation in India during 2007–08 in wheat and rice remained below 11 per cent, whereas global prices show more than 100 per cent inflation in wheat and more than 200 per cent in rice during early months of 2008.

Given India's situation where majority of producers and consumers are vulnerable and not in a position to absorb price shocks, it is vital to maintain a balance between producers' and consumers' interests while using trade policy instruments. The authors highlight that Indian policymakers have moderated transmission of high global prices, which is favourable to producers and adverse for consumers, through checks on export. Conversely, transmission of low interna-

tional prices, which is favourable to consumers but detrimental for the producers, has been moderated through varying tariffs and other checks on imports. Duty on imports is kept low when international prices are high or domestic prices are high and vice versa. Besides trade policy measures, domestic prices are also influenced by the system of minimum support price implemented through public procurement and through open market sales by the Food Corporation of India by liquidating stocks held by it. The underlying logic is to protect consumers from high prices and producers from low prices. The key lesson from India's experience is strategic Liberalization, and regulated trade can be very important policy tools to ensure food security as well as prosperity for producers.

India's growth has often been termed services-led growth as three quarters of the growth is contributed by the services sector. However, contrary to the general belief, it is not trade in services which has acted as the growth engine but domestic demand. Within the services sector, domestic trade, communication services and financial services have recorded high growth rates. While domestic trade and communication services have not been the focus of Liberalization policy, financial services have experienced many policy interventions. Public sector banks played a dominant role, and the government exercised strict control over them through instruments such as cash reserve ratio and statutory liquidity ratio. Rigid regulations ensured that banks offered the government easy and low-cost access to funds and effectively facilitated the implementation of various fiscal policies. The 1991 reforms allowed entry of new private and foreign banks, but unlike in many other countries, these reforms were not triggered by any impending crisis but were indigenously formulated. Also, while market shares of domestic private and foreign banks were permitted to increase, there was no attempt to end government ownership by large-scale privatisation of existing public sector banks. These reforms were primarily designed to introduce "operational flexibility" and functional autonomy in order to improve productivity and efficiency of banks.

The second phase came in 1998, which addressed the question of financial stability of the banking sector. The RBI adopted prudential banking norms consistent with the Basel Accord (1988) and the subsequent Basel II (2004). These reforms introduced significant changes in the Indian banking industry. They increased competition by opening doors to new domestic and foreign banks by allowing private ownership of up to

49 per cent of total equity; 20 per cent of private equity could be held by foreign individuals and financial institutions. In the 2000s, FDI in private banks was allowed up to 75 per cent. An important domestic policy which contributed to improvement of efficiency and competitiveness of the sector was the introduction of a voluntary retirement scheme (VRS) for employees in public sector banks in 2000.

To estimate the impact of Liberalization and other reforms on the Indian banking sector, Subhash C. Ray estimates total factor productivity and technical efficiency of banks during 1992–2009, comparing the performance of public sector banks with that of private domestic banks and foreign banks. The average public sector bank in the data used is over 2.5 times as large as a private bank and more than 9.5 times as large as a foreign bank in terms of deposit or credit. Choosing carefully the most suitable measures of output and inputs, the author finds public sector banks to be the most efficient. Foreign banks come second followed by private banks. Interestingly, public sector banks are found to have improved in efficiency over the years. Foreign banks, on the other hand, start from a higher level of efficiency than public sector banks but become less efficient over subsequent years. Private sector banks are less efficient to start with and become more so in later years. In terms of total factor productivity growth, foreign banks experienced annual growth of 3 per cent, private banks 0.5 per cent and public sector banks only 0.1 per cent. Low productivity growth in the public sector is explainable as public sector banks had higher level of total factor productivity than private or foreign banks and, moreover, State Bank of India (SBI) has been excluded for making the groups more comparable.

It is generally believed that foreign banks have higher efficiency and provide better quality of service by introducing international standards of professionalism in management. However, the Indian experience shows that public sector banks are more efficient. This is possibly due to economies of scale enjoyed by public sector banks. However, the author finds that Indian banks provide better quality of service than foreign banks. During 2009–10, on an average, there were 6 complaints per 100,000 accounts for public sector banks, 18 for private banks, and 51 for foreign banks. Comparing the best banks in the three groups, namely, SBI (public sector bank), ICICI (private sector bank) and HSBC (foreign bank), the author finds that starting from 2001 total factor productivity of SBI took an upward trajectory and continued to grow steadily till the end of the period, 2009. However, the best among the private and foreign banks were more productive than the best public bank. ICICI performed better than foreign banks mostly.

According to the author, an important takeaway from India's experience of banking sector Liberalization is that given an inherent conflict between the objectives of commercial profitability and financial inclusion and universal banking, choosing social objectives may eventually lead to achieving commercial objectives as well. The Liberalization of the banking sector was a deliberate and gradualist attempt to allow private and foreign banks a greater role to improve efficiency through competition. There was no all-out privatisation of public sector banks. Social banking objectives were not discarded to make room for privatisation. However, limited private ownership of government banks made them accountable to shareholders and subject to market discipline. This forced them to regain economic viability through higher productivity and also to retain business by becoming more sensitive to customer needs. Instead of discontinuing the requirement of priority sector lending, the government widened its coverage, giving banks a wider choice in meeting their directed credit obligations. The new guidelines for private banks are designed to ensure competence, prudence and transparency.

Overall, India's experience of Liberalization in agriculture, manufacturing and finance shows that Liberalization has been gradual, voluntary and tailored according to the needs of the economy. The role of the state has been to use markets to not only maximise commercial objectives but also seek to galvanise attempts to attain social objectives. The cautious approach towards Liberalization has provided the state with enough policy space to pursue development-led Liberalization.

REFERENCES

Acharya S (2008). The Rajan Report on Finance. *Business Standard*. April 10.

Ahluwalia MS (1999). Reforming India's Financial Sector: an Overview. In: Hanson JA and Kathuria S, eds. *India: A Financial Sector for the Twenty-First Century*. Oxford University Press. New Delhi.

Ahluwalia MS (2002). Economic reforms in India since 1991: has gradualism worked? *Journal of Economic Perspectives*. 16 (3): 67–88.

Asafu-Adjaye J and Chakraborty D (1999). Export-led growth and import compression: further time series evidence from LDCs. *Australian Economic Papers*. 38: 164–175.

Athukorala P (2009). Outward foreign direct investment from India. *Asian Development Review*. 26(2): 125–153.

Balassa B (1978). Exports and economic growth: further evidence. *Journal of Development Economics*. 5: 181–189.

Banerjee AV *et al.* (2004). Banking reform in India. MIT Working Paper.

Banga R and Kumar D (2011). India's exports of software services: role of external demand and productivity. *Science Technology and Society*. 16: 285–307.

Bardhan P (2005). Nature of opposition to economic reforms in India. *Economic and Political Weekly*. November 26, 2005: 4995–4998.

Bell C and Rousseau PL (2001). Post-independence India: a case of finance-led industrialization? *Journal of Development Economics*. 65 (1): 153–175.

Bhalla GS (2004). *Globalization and Agriculture, State of India's Farmers*, *Millennium Study*. Academic Foundation. New Delhi.

Bhandari L *et al.* (2003). Development financial institutions, financial constraints and growth: evidence from the Indian corporate sector. *Journal of Emerging Market Finance*. 2: 83–121.

Bhatt V and Virmani A (2005). Global integration of India's money market: interest rate parity in India. ICRIER Working Paper, 164.

Bhattacharyya A *et al.* (1997). The impact of liberalization on the productive efficiency of Indian commercial banks. *European Journal of Operational Research*. 98: 332–345.

Chakraborty L (2008). Analysing the Raghuram Rajan Committee Report on financial sector reforms. *Economic & Political Weekly*. 21.

Chakravarty S and Singh A (1988). The desirable forms of economic openness in the South. *WIDER Discussion Paper*. Helsinki.

Chand R (2003). *Government Intervention in Foodgrain Markets in India in the Changing Context*. Policy Paper 19, National Centre for Agricultural Economics and Policy Research. New Delhi.

Chand R (2008). International trade, food security and the response to the WTO in South Asian countries. In: Khasnobis BG *et al.*, eds. *Food Security; Indicators, Measurement and the Impact of Trade Openness*. Oxford University Press. UK.

Chand R (1999a). Effects of trade Liberalization on agriculture in India: commodity aspects. Working Paper, 45, CGPRT Centre, ESCAP, United Nations. Bogor, Indonesia, 1999.

Chand R (1999b). Trade Liberalization and net social welfare: a Study of selected crops. *Economic and Political Weekly*. 34(52), 25 December: A153 – A159.

Chand R (2002a). Indian agriculture and WTO: looking beyond Doha. Keynote Paper, IX Annual Conference Proceedings. *Agricultural Economics Research Review*. 17–42, 2002.

Chand R (2002b). *Trade Liberalization, WTO and Indian Agriculture: Experience and Prospects.* Mittal Publications. New Delhi.

Chand R (2007). Wheat import and price outlook for 2007–08: separating the grain from the chaff, *Economic and Political Weekly.* 42 (30): 3196–3199.

Chand R (2009). Global food and financial crises: experience and perspectives from India. In: *Agricultural Reforms and Trade Liberalization in China and Selected Asian Countries: Lessons of Three Decades*, *Policy Assistance Series 6*. FAO Regional Office for Asia and the Pacific. RAP Publication. 2009/15, Bangkok.

Chand R and Kumar P (2006). Country case study India. In: Thomas H, ed. *Trade Reforms and Food Security*. Food and Agriculture Organization of United Nations. Rome: 329–364.

Chand R *et al.* (2004). WTO and oilseeds sector. *Economic and Political Weekly.* 7 February, 39 (6): 533–537.

Chand R and Jha D (2001). Trade liberalization: agricultural prices and net social welfare. In: Acharya SS and Chaudhari DP, eds. *Indian Agricultural Policy at the Cross Roads.* Rawat Publishers. New Delhi.

Chandra R (2002). Export growth and economic growth: an investigation of causality in India. *Indian Economic Journal.* 49 (3): 64–73.

Cho YJ and Khatkhate D (1989). Financial Liberalization: issues and evidence. *Economic and Political Weekly.* 20 May.

Chow PCY (1987). Causality between export growth and industrial development: empirical evidence from the NICs. *Journal of Development Economics.* 26: 55–63.

Clemente J *et al.* (1998). Testing for a unit root in variables with a double change in the mean. *Economics Letters.* 59 (1998): 175–182.

Das A *et al.* (2005). Liberalization, ownership, and efficiency in Indian banking: a nonparametric approach. *Economic and Political Weekly*. 19 March: 1190–1197.

Das A and Ghosh S. (2006). Financial deregulation and efficiency: an empirical analysis of Indian banks during the post-reform period. *Review of Financial Economics*. 15: 193–221.

Das DK (2003). Manufacturing productivity under varying trade regimes: India in the 1980s and 1990s. Working Paper No. 107, ICRIER. New Delhi.

Das SK. (2010). Financial liberalization and banking sector efficiency: the Indian experience. Paper presented at the 12th Money and Finance Conference. IGIDR. Mumbai, 11–12 March.

Deaton A and Dreze J (2009). Food and nutrition in India: facts and interpretations. *Economic and Political Weekly*. 44 (7): 42–64.

Dhawan U and Biswal B (1999). Re-examining export led growth hypothesis: multivariate cointegration analysis for India. *Applied Economics*. 31: 525–530.

Dholkia B H (1997). Impact of economic Liberalization on the growth of Indian agriculture. In: Desai BM, ed. *Agricultural Development Paradigm for the Ninth Plan under New Economic Environment*. Oxford and IBH Publishing Co. Pvt. Ltd. New Delhi.

Diamond DW and Dybvig PH (1983). Bank runs, deposit insurance, and liquidity. *Journal of Political Economy*. 91 (June): 401–419.

Diaz-Alejandro C (1985). Good-bye financial repression, hello financial crash. *Journal of Development Economics*. 19: 1–24.

Echeverri-Gent J (2007). Politics of market micro structure: towards a new political economy of India's equity market reform. In: Mukherjee R., ed. *India's Economic Transition: The Politics of Reforms*. Oxford University Press. New Delhi.

Emran MS and Stiglitz JE (2008). Financial liberalization, financial restraint, and entrepreneurial development. Working Paper, Columbia University, available at www.aeaweb.org/assa/2009/retrieve.php?pdfid=448.

Ghatak S and Price SW (1997). Export composition and economic growth: cointegration and causality evidence for India. *Weltwirtschaftliches Archiv.* 133 (3): 538–553.

Ghosh A (2006). Pathways through financial crisis: India. *Global Governance.* 12: 413–429.

Giovannini A (1985). Saving and the real interest rate in LDCs. *Journal of Development Economics.* 18: 197–217.

Gokarn S (2001). The financial sector. In: National Council of Applied Economic Research (NCAER), *The Economic and Policy Reform in India.* Delhi.

Goldar B (2002). TFP growth in the Indian manufacturing in the 1980s. *Economic and Political Weekly.* 37(49): 4966–4968.

Goldar B and Kumari A (2003). Import liberalization and productivity growth in Indian manufacturing industries in the 1990s. *Developing Economies.* December, 41(4): 436–460.

Goldar B and Mitra A (2002). Total factor productivity growth in Indian industry: a review of studies. In: Minhas BS, ed. *National Income Accounts and Data Systems.* Oxford University Press. New Delhi.

Gopinath S (2011). Approach to capital account management – shifting contours. Keynote

Address by Deputy Governor, RBI at the Annual Conference of the Foreign Exchange Dealers'Association of India (FEDAI) on 18 February 2011 at Thimpu.

Government of India (1998). *Report of the Committee on Banking Sector Reforms* (Chairman: Narasimham M). New Delhi. Government of India.

Government of India (2005). *Report of the High Level Expert Committee on Corporate Bonds and Securitization* (Chairman: Patil RH). New Delhi. Government of India.

Government of India (2007). *Report of the High Powered Expert Committee on Making Mumbai an International Financial Centre.* Sage Publications. New Delhi.

Government of India (2011): *Report of the Committee on Comprehensive Review of National Small Savings Fund* (Chairperson: Gopinath S). New Delhi. Government of India.

Government of India (2008). *A Hundred Small Steps: Report of the Committee on Financial Sector Reforms* (Chairman: Rajan R). New Delhi. Planning Commission, Government of India.

Granger CWJ (1969). Investigating causal relations by econometric models and cross-spectral methods. *Econometrica.* 37: 424–438.

Greenaway D and Sapsford D (1994). Exports, growth, and liberalization: an evaluation. *Journal of Policy Modelling.* 16: 165–186.

Grossman GM and Helpman E (1991). *Innovation and Growth in the Global Economy.* MIT Press. Cambridge, MA.

Gulati A (2001). *Trade Liberalization and Food Security: Challenges to Indian Policy Makers* (mimeo). International Food Policy Research Institute (IFPRI). Washington DC. January.

Gulati A (2002). Indian agriculture in a globalizing world. *American Journal of Agricultural Economics.* 84 (3): 754–761.

Gulati A and Sharma A (1994). Agricultural under GATT: what it holds for India. *Economic and Political Weekly.* 29 (29): 1857–1863.

Gulati A and Sharma A (1995). Subsidy syndrome in Indian agriculture. *Economic and Political Weekly.* 30, 30 September.

Gulati A and Sharma A (1997). Freeing trade in agriculture: implications for resource use efficiency and cropping pattern changes. *Economic and Political Weekly*. 32 (52): A154–A164. 27 December.

Gulati A *et al.* (1996). Self-sufficiency and allocative efficiency – case of edible oils. *Economic and Political Weekly*. 30 March.

Gupta P *et al.* (2011). Bank ownership and the effects of financial liberalization: evidence from India. IMF Working Paper WP/11/50.

Gurley JG and Shaw ES (1955). Financial aspects of economic development. *American Economic Review*. 45: 515–538.

Hashim DA *et al.* (2009). Impact of major liberalization on productivity: the J-curve hypothesis. Working Paper No. 5/2009-DEA. Ministry of Finance, Government of India.

Islam MN (1998). Export expansion and economic growth: testing for cointegration and causality. *Applied Economics*. 30: 415–425.

Jha S and Srinivasan PV (1999). Grain price stabilization in India: evaluation of policy alternatives. *Agricultural Economics*. 21 (1): 93–108.

Joshi V (2003). India and the Impossible Trinity. *World Economy*. 26, April: 555–583.

Jung SW and Marshall PJ (1985). Exports, growth and causality in developing countries. *Journal of Development Economics*. 18: 1–12.

Kasahara H and Rodrigue J (2008). Does the use of imported intermediates increase productivity? Plant-level evidence. *Journal of Development Economics*. 87: 106–118.

Ketkar KW and Ketkar SL (2008). Performance and profitability of Indian banks in the post liberalization period. Paper presented at the 2008 World Congress on National Accounts and Economic Performance Measures for Nations. Washington DC. 13–17 May 2008.

Khambata F and Khambata D (1989). Emerging capital markets: a case study of equity markets in India. *Journal of Developing Areas*. 23: 425–438.

Kumari (2010). Liberalization and sources of industrial growth in India: an analysis based on input-output approach. Working Paper, IEG. New Delhi.

Kumbhakar SC and Sarkar S (2003). Deregulation, ownership and productivity growth in the banking industry: evidence from India. *Journal of Money, Credit, and Banking*. 35: 403–414.

Levine R (2005). Finance and growth: theory and evidence. In: Aghion P and Durlauf S, eds. *Handbook of Economic Growth*. Volume 1: 865–934. Amsterdam. North Holland.

Singh M (1995). Inaugural address delivered at the 54th Annual Conference of the Indian Society of Agricultural Economics. *Indian Journal of Agricultural Economics*. 50 (1), January–March.

McKinnon RI (1973). *Money and Capital in Economic Development*. Brookings Institution. Washington DC.

Meenakshi JV and Vishwanathan B (2003). Calorie deprivation in rural India, 1983–1999/2000. *Economic and Political Weekly*. 36 (4): 369–375.

Mohan R (2004a). Financial sector reforms in India: policies and performance analysis. *Reserve Bank of India Bulletin*. October.

Mohan R (2004b). Ownership and governance in private sector banks in India. *Reserve Bank of India Bulletin*. October: 879–883.

Mohan, R (2005). Reforms, productivity, and efficiency in banking: the Indian experience. *The Pakistan Development Review*. 44 (4):505–538.

Mohan R (2009). *Monetary Policy in a Globalized Economy.* Oxford University Press. New Delhi.

Mohan R and Kapur M (2011). Managing the impossible trinity: volatile capital flows and Indian monetary policy. In: Mohan R, ed. *Growth with Financial Stability.* Oxford University Press. New Delhi.

Rakesh R and Ray P (2011). Development of the Indian debt market. In: Mohan R, ed. *Growth with Financial Stability.* Oxford University Press. New Delhi.

Narashimham Committee (1992). Report of the Committee on the Financial System. *Reserve Bank of India Bulletin.* February: 369–380.

National Council of Applied Economic Research (NCAER) – EPW Research Foundation (EPWRF) (2003). *Household Savings and Investment Behaviour in India.* NCAER. Delhi.

Nayyar D and Sen A (1994a). International Trade and Agricultural Sector in India. In: Bhalla GS, ed. *Economic Liberalization and Indian Agriculture.* Institute for Studies in Industrial Development. New Delhi.

Nayyar D and Sen A (1994b). International trade and the agricultural in India. *Economic and Political Weekly.* 29 (20).

Ostry J and Reinhart CM (1992). Private saving and terms of trade shocks: evidence from developing countries. *International Monetary Fund Staff Papers.* 39: 495–517.

Panda M and Quizon J (2001). Growth and distribution under trade liberalization in India. In: Guha A *et al.,* eds. *Trade and Industry: Essays by NIPFP-Ford Foundation Fellows.* National Institute of Public Finance and Policy. New Delhi.

Parikh KS *et al.* (1997). Agricultural trade liberalization: growth, welfare and large country effects. *Agricultural Economics.* 17 (1): 1–20.

Parikh K *et al.* (1995). Strategies for agricultural Liberalization: consequences for growth, welfare and distribution. *Economic and Political Weekly.* 30 September.

Patel IG (2002). *Glimpses of Indian Economic Policy: An Insider's View.* Oxford University Press. New Delhi.

Patil RH (2001). Broadbasing and deepening the bond market in India. Wharton Financial Institutions Center Working Paper. 1–32.

Perron P and Vogelsang TJ (1992). Testing for a unit root in a time series with a changing mean: corrections and extensions. *Journal of Business & Economic Statistics.* 10 October: 467–470.

Portela MCS and Thanassoulis E (2005). Profitability of a sample of Portuguese bank branches and its decomposition into technical and allocative components. *European Journal of Operational Research.* 162 (3): 850–866.

Portela MCS and Thanassoulis E (2007). Malmquist indexes using a geometric distance function (GDF). Application to a sample of Portuguese bank branches. *Journal of Productivity Analysis.* 2007.

Pradhan NC (2010). Exports and economic growth: an examination of ELG hypothesis for India. *Reserve Bank of India Occasional Papers.* 31 (3).

Pursell G and Gulati A (1995). Liberalising Indian agriculture: an agenda for reform. In: Cassen R and Joshi V, eds. *India: The Future of Economic Reform.* Oxford University Press. Oxford/New Delhi.

Mohan TTR and Ray SC (2003). Productivity and efficiency at public and private banks in India. Paper presented at the Fifth Annual Conference on Money and Finance in the Indian Economy. Indira Gandhi Institute of Development Research. Mumbai.

Mohan TTR and Ray SC (2004). Comparing performance of public and private sector banks: a revenue maximization efficiency approach. *Economic and Political Weekly.* 39 (12): 1271–1276.

Ram R (1987). Exports and economic growth in developing countries: evidence from time series and cross-section data. *Economic Development and Cultural Change.* 36: 51–72.

Rana PB (1986). Exports and economic growth: further evidence from Asian LDCs. *Pakistan Journal of Applied Economics.* 5: 163–178.

Rangarajan C (2009). *India: Monetary Policy, Financial Stability and Other Essays.* Academic Foundation. New Delhi.

Rangarajan C (2007). The Indian banking system – challenges ahead. Speech delivered at the Indian Institute of Bankers.

Rao CHH and Ashok A (1994). Indian agriculture: emerging perspective and policy issues. *Economic and Political Weekly.* 31 December, 29 (53): A158–A170.

Rao VM (1994). Agriculture and Liberalization: some implications for development policies. *Economic and Political Weekly.* 16/23 April, 29 (16/17): 999–1004.

Ray SC and Das A (2010). Distribution of cost and profit efficiency: evidence from Indian banking. *European Journal of Operational Research.* 201 (1): 297–307.

Ray SC and Chen L (2011). A normative interpretation of the Tornqvist Productivity Index. Paper presented at the 9th International Conference on DEA at Thessaloniki, Greece, August 2011.

Reddy YV (2004). Monetary and financial sector reforms in India: a practitioner's perspective. In: Kaushik B, ed. *India's Emerging Economy: Performance and Prospects in the 1990s and Beyond.* The M.I.T. Press. Cambridge, Massachusetts.

Reddy YV (2000). *Monetary and Financial Sector Reforms in India.* UBSPD Publishers. New Delhi.

Reddy YV (2009). *India and the Global Financial Crisis: Managing Money and Finance.* Orient Blackswan. Hyderabad.

Reddy YV (2002). Public sector banks and the governance challenge: Indian experience. Lecture delivered at the World Bank, IMF and Brookings Institutions Conference, April 2002.

Reddy YV (1998). Managing capital flows. Presentation at the seminar at Asia/Pacific Research Centre, Stanford University, 23 November 1998. Available at http://www.rbi.org.in.

Reinhart CM and Sbrancia MB (2011). The Liquidation of Government Debt. NBER Working Paper. No. 16893. Available at http://www.nber.org/papers/w16893.

Reserve Bank of India (1985). *Report of the Committee to Review the Working of the Monetary System* (Chairman: Chakravarty S). Reserve Bank of India. Mumbai.

Reserve Bank of India (1987). *Report of the Working Group on the Money Market* (Chairman: Vaghul N). Reserve Bank of India. Mumbai.

Reserve Bank of India (1991). *Report of the Committee on the Financial System* (Chairman: Narasimham M). Reserve Bank of India. Mumbai.

Reserve Bank of India (1995). *Report on Foreign Exchange Markets in India* (Chairman: Sodhani OP). Reserve Bank of India. Mumbai.

Reserve Bank of India (2002). *Report on Currency and Finance, 2001.* Mumbai.

Reserve Bank of India (2004). *Report on Currency and Finance, 2002–03.* Mumbai.

Reserve Bank of India (2007). *Report on Currency and Finance, 2005–06.* Mumbai.

Reserve Bank of India (2008). *Reports on Currency and Finance, 2003–08, Volume IV (The Banking Sector in India: Emerging Issues and Challenges).* Mumbai.

Reserve Bank of India (2009). *Report of the Working Group on Benchmark Prime Lending Rate* (BPLR) (Chairman: Mohanty D). Mumbai.

Reserve Bank of India (2010). *Report on Trend and Progress of Banking in India 2010*. Mumbai.

Reserve Bank of India (2010). *Statistical Tables Relating to Banks in India 2009–10.*. Mumbai.

Riezman RG *et al.* (1996). The engine of growth or its handmaiden? A time series assessment of export-led growth. *Empirical Economics*. 21: 77–113.

Rossi N (1988). Government spending, the real interest rate, and the behaviour of liquidity constrained consumers in developing countries. *International Monetary Fund Staff Papers*. 35: 104–140.

Sahu S and Virmani A (2005). Structure of the Household Asset Portfolios in India. ICRIER Working Paper. 157.

Sarkar SJ *et al.* (2008). Does ownership always matter? evidence from the Indian banking industry. *Journal of Comparative Economics*. 26: 262–281.

Sen K and Vaidya RR (1997). *The Process of Financial Liberalization in India.* Oxford University Press. New Delhi.

Sensarma R (2006). Are foreign banks always the best? Comparison of state-owned, private and foreign banks in India. *Economic Modelling*. 23: 717–735.

Shah A and Patnaik I (2011). Reforming the Indian financial system. Working Paper 2011-80. National Institute of Public Finance and Policy. New Delhi.

Shammugam KR and Das A (2004). Efficiency of Indian commercial banks during the reform period. *Applied Financial Economics*. 14: 681–686.

Shaw E (1973). *Financial Deepening in Economic Development.* Oxford University Press. New York.

Shetty SL (2007). India's saving performance since the advent of planning: an eclectic review and design of policy for promoting domestic savings. In: Vaidyanathan A and Krishna KL, eds. *Institutions and Markets in India's Development*. Oxford University Press. Delhi.

Shetty SL and Ray P (2011). The evolving contours of monetary policy and commercial banking in India. Review on Indian monetary policy submitted as a research survey to the Indian Council of Social Science Research.

Srivastava DK (2012). Indian economy: role of services sector, mimeo, Madras School of Economics.

Srinivasan PV and Jha S (1999). Food security through price stabilization: buffer stocks vs variable levies. *Economic and Political Weekly*. 20 November, 34 (46–47): 3299–3304.

Stiglitz JE and Weiss A (1981). Credit rationing in markets with imperfect information. *American Economic Review*. 71: 393–410.

Stiglitz JE (1999). Lessons from East Asia. Remarks at the Symposium of Institute for International Monetary Affairs on "Recovery of the World Economy".

Storm S (1997). Agriculture under trade policy reform: a quantitative assessment for India. *World Development*. March, 25 (3): 425–436.

Storm S (2001). The desirable form of openness for Indian agriculture. *Cambridge Journal of Economics*. 25: 185–207.

Subbarao D (2009). Global financial crisis: questioning the questions. JRD Tata Memorial Lecture delivered at the meeting of The Associated Chambers of Commerce and Industry of India, New Delhi on 31 July 2009.

Trivedi *et al.* (2011). Productivity, efficiency and competitiveness of the Indian manufacturing sector. Reserve Bank of India. Mumbai.

Virmani A (1982). The nature of credit markets in developing countries. World Bank Staff Working Paper. 525.

Virmani A (1992a). Partial rupee convertibility (PCR): a free market exchange rate channel. January.

Virmani A (1992b). Trends in current account deficit and the balance of trade: separating facts from prejudices. *Journal of Foreign Exchange and International Finance*. April–June 1992, 6 (1): 72–78.

Virmani A (1992c). Partial convertibility of the rupee (PCR) implications for exporters. *RBI Bulletin.* August: 1300–1302.

Virmani A (2001). India's 1990–91 crisis: reforms, myths and paradoxes. Planning Commission Working Paper No. 4/2001-PC. December. (http://www.planningcommission.nic.in/reports/wrkpapers/wp_cris9091.pdf).

Virmani A (2003). India's external reforms: modest globalization significant gains. *Economic and Political Weekly.* 9–15 August, 37 (32): 3373–3390.

Virmani A (2006a). India's economic growth history: fluctuations. trends, break points and phases. *Indian Economic Review.* January–June, 41 (1): 81–103.

Virmani A (2006b), The dynamics of competition: phasing of domestic and external Liberalization in India, Planning Commission Working Paper, No. 4/2006-PC.

Virmani A (2007). Macro-economic management of Indian economy: capital flows, interest rates and inflation. DEA Working paper No. 2/2007-DEA. Ministry of Finance, Government of India. November. http://finmin.nic.in/WorkingPaper/index.html.

Virmani A (2009). *The Sudoku of India's Growth.* BS Books. New Delhi.

Virmani A (2009b). Macro-economic management of the Indian economy: capital flows, interest rates and inflation. *Macroeconomics and Finance in Emerging Market Economies.* September, 2 (2): 189–214.

Virmani A and Hashim DA (2009). Factor employment, sources and sustainability of output growth: analysis of Indian manufacturing. DEA Working Paper No. 3/2009-DEA. Ministry of Finance, Government of India.

Virmani A and Hashim DA (2011). J-curve of productivity and growth: Indian manufacturing post-liberalization. IMF Working Paper WP/11/163.

Wallack JS (2003). Structural breaks in Indian macroeconomic data. *Economic & Political Weekly.* 38: 4312–4315.

Wells S and Schou-Zibell L (2008). India's bond market – developments and challenges ahead. ADB Working Paper Series on Regional Economic Integration No. 22.

NOTES

1   United Nations' World Economic Situations and Prospects 2012 report.

2   Source: Government of India, Economic Survey 2011,

3   Banga and Kumar (2011)

4   D.K. Srivastava (2011)

5   UNCTAD Information Economy Report 2009.

6   UNCTAD Information Economy Report 2010.

7   Source: Central Statistical Organization, National Accounts Statistics.

8   Tendulkar (2000).

9   Deflated by Export Unit Value Index.

10 Exports are deflated by export unit value index and imports by import unit value index with 1978–79 as base year. Data for exports and imports of manufactured products is drawn from Reserve Bank of India, *Handbook of Statistics*.

11 A cross check on the growth was undertaken using ratio of manufacture exports and imports to total merchandise exports and imports from World Development Indicators. This ratio was applied to India's merchandise exports/imports in local currency. The current price series arrived at was deflated be export/import unit value indices. The trend appeared to be the same.

12 http://indiabudget.nic.in/es2010-11/echap-01.pdf.

13 See Perron 2006 ; Perron and Volelsang 1992 for the underlying models estimated.

14 which assumes instantaneous changes in intercept;

15 which assumes a gradual change in the intercept and/or slope. The change persists in its effects beyond the initial shock.

16 Data provided by *Economic and Political Weekly*.

17 Chamarbagwala and Sharma (2008), *Industrial De-Licensing, Trade Liberalization, and Skill Upgradation in India*.

18 Inclusion of imports also helps in avoiding spurious causality result; see Riezman and Summers (1996).

19 Data for a longer comparable time series is not available from ASI. Many studies have estimated Granger causality and cointegration analysis based on around 30 years of annual data (e.g. Sharma and Panagiotidis, 2005 reinvestigated economic growth sources in India for the periods 1971 to 2000; Asafu-Adjaye *et al.* (1999) tests ELG for the period 1960-1994; Ghatak and Price (1997) tests the ELG hypothesis for India during 1960-1992. An alternative specification is also tried with a longer time series.

20 The series built by Virmani and Hashim (2011) has been used.

21 For details of the results see Banga and Das (2011), MPRA Paper No. 35198.

22 For details of the results see Banga and Das (2011), MPRA Paper No. 35198.

23 Under the new economic policy, rupee was devalued by 18 per cent against dollar and exchange rate was left to be determined by market forces. The new Export-Import Policy for 1992/1997 was announced for five years instead of three in the past. The main features of the policy were that trade was free except for a small negative lists of imports and exports. Canalization of trade was abandoned and government stopped determining the value or nature of the import or exports, except for exports of onion and import of cereals, pulses and edible oils. Most of the quantitative restrictions on agricultural trade flows were dismantled and tariff was also lowered somewhat.

24 Use of GDP or value added as the denominator for estimating openness, as is the common practice, overestimates the degree of openness. Since export/import represent value of output rather than value added it is proper to use value of domestic production rather than GDP as denominator to estimate extent of integration of domestic economy with world economy.

25 In fact after mid-1980s, growth rate in oilseeds production was higher than that in food grains (Chand *et al.* 2004).

26 Oilseeds in India are used to produce oil and oil meal and cake. While almost all the vegetable oil is consumed in the domestic market, a large share of the oil meal, which is a very rich source of protein, is exported. From 2004–05 to 2008–09, India exported more than 6 million tonne of oilcake annually.

27 For details, see Chand (2009).

28 See Sen and Vaidya (1997), Reddy (2000), Ahluwalia (2003), Rangarajan (2009), and Mohan (2009) on the salient features of Indian financial Liberalization.

29 Interestingly, Cho and Khatkhate observed, "One of the most important lessons to be drawn from financial Liberalization across countries is that price stability and, more broadly, macro-economic stability, is the linchpin of successful Liberalization, not the deregulation of interest rates *per se,* especially when the countries undergoing financial reforms have shallow financial markets" (p. 1111).

30 Bank nationalization was essentially a political decision. It is instructive to note what I.G. Patel, then Secretary of Economic Affairs of Ministry of Finance, said in his autobiography, "It was, I think, later in July 1969 that I was sent for once again. No one else was present. Without any fanfare, she (the Late Mrs. Indira Gandhi, the then Prime Minister) asked me whether banking was under my charge. On my telling that it was, she simply said: 'For political reasons, it has been decided to nationalise the banks....' There was no pretence that this was a political decision." (Patel, 2002; p. 135).

31 Estimated over 1980– 2009 (i.e., 30-year annual data), the household saving equation emerges as follows:
$$(S_h/Y)_t = 1.017 + 0.001*GPDI_t - 0.011*Depend_t - 0.004*i_t - 0.0003*PCI_t + 0.0036*BankPop_t + 0.3679*(S_h/Y)_{t-1}$$
$$(4.19)\# \quad (1.64)@@ \quad (3.83)\# \quad (2.61)* \quad (3.57)\# \quad (2.19)@ \quad (2.31)@$$

with $R^2 = 0.957$; DW = 1.77; figures in parentheses are *t* values, #, @, and @@ indicate significance at 1 percent, 5 and 10 per cent, respectively, and S_h is household savings, Y is GDP, GPDI is growth of personal disposable income, Depend is old age dependency ratio, i is the interest rate, PCI is the per capita income, BankPop is population per bank branch.

32 Athukorala and Sen (2004) concluded, "Bank density stands out to be a highly significant variable in explaining variations in the private saving rate. A 10% decline in population per bank branch seems to increase the private saving rate by 0.4 percentage points".

33 We are unable to run the equation, reported in footnote (7), with a nationalization dummy because of paucity of reliable data on all variables needed.

34 Illustratively, Giovannini (1985) found that in only 5 of the 18 developing countries in his sample saving turned out to be sensitive to changes in the real interest rate. Rossi (1988) also found that increases in the real rate of return are not likely to elicit substantial increases in savings, especially in low-income developing countries. In a model with a single consumption good, Ostry and Reinhart (1992) confirm these findings but when a disaggregated commodity structure that allows for traded and non-traded goods is assumed, these authors find higher and statistically significant estimates of the intertemporal elasticity of substitution.

35 Bell and Rousseau (2002) concluded their study on growth-finance relationship in India as, "For India, at least, it appears that a particular form of financial development, whatever its flaws, has played an important role in the industrialization process" (p. 172).

36 To identify the importance of nationalization on domestic savings a more thorough empirical analysis is needed, with a model containing demographic and macro variables along with a nationalization dummy! Similarly we need to examine the effect of nationalization on capital deepening, a commonly used measure of which is the Private credit to GDP ratio.

37 These institutions comprised all-India development banks such as Industrial Development Bank of India, Industrial Credit and Investment Corporation of India, Industrial Finance Corporation of India, Industrial Investment Corporation of India, and Small Industries Development Bank of India. Specialised institutions such as Risk Capital & Technology Finance Corporation (later turned into IFCI Venture Capital Funds), investment institutions such as UTI, LIC and GIC and its subsidiaries and state-level institutions such as SFCs and SIDCs.

38 Before we move to the post 1990 phase of economic Liberalization, it may be noted that seeds of economic Liberalization were already sown in early 1980s (Virmani, 2009).

39 As an ex-Governor of the Reserve Bank of India put it, "By the end of the eighties, the financial system was considerably stretched. The directed and concessional availability of bank credit with respect to certain sectors resulted not only in distorting the interest rate mechanism, but also adversely affected the viability and profitability of banks. The lack of recognition of the importance of transparency, accountability and prudential norms in the operations of the banking system led also to a rising burden of nonperforming assets" (Reddy, 2004).

40 See Sen and Vaidya (1997), Ahluwalia (1999), Reddy (2000), Rangarajan (2009), and Mohan (2009) on the broad contours of Indian financial Liberalization.

41   Narasimam Committee I also recommended phasing out of directed credit programs, which was not accepted.

42   Small Savings Schemes in India date back to 1882 when Post Office Savings Bank, which were designated as Government Savings Banks, was started to encourage habit of savings.

43   Major Liberalization unleashes competitive pressures that can dramatically change the relative profitability of various activities and institutions. The conventional analysis emphasizes the positive effects of competition on productivity (through adoption of new technology) and growth. There is also a short-run negative effect arising from obsolescence and diversion of resources to new learning that can overwhelm the positive effect and produce a down ward kink in growth and productivity, before the positive effect becomes strong (J)-Virmani(2005, 2011).

44   Out of these, four were promoted by financial institutions, one each by conversion of co-operative bank and NBFC into commercial banks, and the remaining six by individual banking professionals and an established media house.

45   There is considerable literature on the relationship between bank ownership and bank efficiency/productivity in India; see Ray (2011) in this volume for an extensive discussion and an up-to-date technical assessment of this issue.

46   Entities / groups having significant (10 per cent or more) income or assets or both from real estate construction and / or broking activities individually or taken together in the last three years will not be eligible.

47   Shareholding by NOHC in excess of 40 per cent shall be brought down to 20 per cent within 10 years and to 15 per cent within 12 years from the date of licensing of the bank.

48   There are other conditions as well. These include (a) exposure of bank to any entity in the promoter group shall not exceed 10 per cent and aggregate exposure to all the entities in the group shall not exceed 20 per cent of the paid-up capital and reserves of the bank; (b) the bank shall get its shares listed on the stock exchanges within two years of licensing; (c) the bank shall open at least 25 per cent of its branches in unbanked rural centres (population up to 9,999 as per 2001 census); and (d) existing NBFCs, if considered eligible, may be permitted to either promote a new bank or convert themselves into banks.

49   Bhandari et al. (2003) evaluated the role of DFIs in India for the period 1989-97 by examining how firms' investment decisions are affected by their ability to access DFIs and found that firms that had prior access to DFIs continue to receive funds from these sources only if they can be classified as a priori more financially constrained.

50   Still a number of development banks remain under complete Government control, viz., SIDBI, Exim Bank, NHB and NABARD.

51   SBI Mutual Fund was the first non-UTI Mutual Fund established in June 1987 followed by Canbank Mutual Fund (December 1987), Punjab National Bank Mutual Fund (Aug 1989), Indian Bank Mutual Fund (Nov 1989), Bank of India (Jun 1990), Bank of Baroda Mutual Fund (Oct 1992). LIC established its mutual fund in June 1989 while GIC had set up its mutual fund in December 1990. Interestingly, most of the subsidiaries of public sector banks are run like private sector commercial companies with market-driven incentive structure.

52   The Specified Undertaking of Unit Trust of India, functioning under an administrator and under the rules framed by Government of India and does not come under the purview of the Mutual Fund Regulations.

53   See Patil (2001), Mohan (2004) and Government of India (2009) for details of reforms in financial markets in India.

54   In May 2011, based on the Report of the Working Group on Monetary policy operating procedures (Chairman: Deepak Mohanty), the Reserve Bank introduced the weighted average overnight call money rate as the new operating target of monetary policy. The repo rate is the only one independently varying policy rate.

55   CBLOs are sort of tripartite repo that allow market participants to create borrowing facilities by placing collateral securities at the CCIL. CBLOs are an innovative technique unique to India (Wells and Schou-Zibell, 2008).

56   The difference between the two can be attributed to the existence of an exchange risk premium over and above the expected depreciation of the currency.

57   Tap issuances, for which the coupon rate was pre-determined but the amount was not notified, were also conducted from time to time up to 2000.

58   As on 30 June 2010, there were 20 Primary Dealers (PDs), of which 12 were banks carrying on Primary Dealership business departmentally (Bank-PDs) and the remaining 8 were non-bank entities, known as standalone PDs, registered as NBFCs under section 45 IA of the RBI Act, 1934.

59   In the Ministry of Finance, Virmani developed and spelt out a new approach to foreign exchange management in a series of internal notes and policy papers, some of which were subsequently made public, including (https://sites.google.com/

site/drarvindvirmani/)"Capital Inflows: Problem or Opportunity", February 1994; "Managing the Exchange Rate: Political Uncertainty, Fundamentals and Expectations", November 1995; "A New Foreign Exchange Act (FEA)", Chintan Policy Paper No. 3, June 1997; "Exchange Rate Management", Chintan Policy Paper No. 5, December 1997; and "Capital Account Convertibility: Timing and Phasing," Chintan Policy Paper No. 16, December 1999.

60   See Echeverri-Gent (2007) for a political economy-related discussion on the establishment of the NSE and corporatization of BSE.

61   For example, *Report of the High Powered Expert Committee on Making Mumbai an International Financial Centre* (Government of India, 2007) noted: "The convertibility question is critically linked to the possibility of a currency crisis, which India has successfully avoided .... This discussion needs to be illuminated by three key points. First, the present Indian policy configuration is not a 'consistent' one, given a pegged exchange rate and attempts at having an autonomous monetary policy while having significant capital account openness. This has, in the past, led to potentially destabilising one-way bets for foreign capital. Second, it is clear that if IFS (international financial services) export is the goal, this is incompatible with capital controls. Third, the growing integration of India into the world on the current account and the capital account is giving de facto convertibility in any case." (p. xxxvii).

62   The sentiment to akin to Stiglitz, who said: "Rapid financial and capital account Liberalization - without the commensurate strengthening of regulatory institutions and safety nets - exposes countries to high levels of risk that they are ill-prepared to absorb. The benefits of the Liberalization, especially in countries with high savings rate, are limited, and further qualified by the costs of the disruptions that they are likely to experience. While capital account Liberalization, through diversification, is supposed to facilitate growth at the same time that it reduces risk, in practice it seems to be associated with higher levels of risk without commensurate increases in growth or investment." (Stiglitz, 1999).

63   Specifically, Tarapore I proposed the some pre-assigned targets on the following variables: Centre's gross fiscal deficit, inflation, gross NPAs of banking sector, cash reserve ratio, debt-Servicing ratio, and current account deficit.

64   Illustratively, Shah and Patnaik (2011) commented: "India has had a highly limited opening of the capital account .... The Chinn-Ito measure (Chinn and Ito, 2008) reports that India has had a constant score on de jure openness at -1.10, at a time when the world average went from -0.378 in 1970 to +0.495 in 2007. This is because India's capital account opening has been characterised by quantitative restrictions, bureaucratic procedures, limitations upon rule of law and complex forms of legal risk".

65   For example, it has been observed, "In the discussion of economic reforms in academia as well as the media in India one finds a wide gulf between the opposing sides, and in some quarters there are even signs of increasing polarization. Each side describes the other in stereotypes and usually talks past each other. The pro-reformers identify the opposition as belonging to the "loony left", caught in a time warp, oblivious of global changes and elementary economics. The other side paints the reform-mongers as "neo-liberal" (a widely used term of abuse in certain circles) and lackeys of global capitalism oblivious of the poor and the dispossessed. Beyond these stereotypes there, mercifully, exist good many people who have problems with both extreme positions, and, of course, they themselves are somewhat divided" (Bardhan, 2005; p. 4995).

66   Also see Chakraborty (2008).

67   Other important studies of efficiency in Indian banking include Shammugam and Das (2004), Sensarma (2006), Das and Ghosh (2009), Zhao, Casu, and Ferrari (2009), and Das (2010).

68   Other variants of the *intermediation approach* are the *user cost approach*, where a financial product is classified as an input or an output based on its net contribution to the revenue of the bank, and the *value added approach*, where deposits and loans are treated as outputs due to their significant contribution to the total value added.

69   Given its dominant position in the Indian banking industry, SBI is likely to unduly influence the performance of public sector banks as a group relative to the other two ownership categories context SBI is a mega bank that by itself accounted for nearly a quarter of the total assets of all the 93 scheduled commercial banks in India in 2000. For this reason, in computing the different efficiency measures, SBI was removed from the data set.

70   This is "optimal" only in a special sense because deposits are maintained at their actual levels.

71   For details see Ray, S.C. "Impact of Liberalization and Globalization on Productivity in Indian Banking: A Comparative Analysis of Public Sector, Private and Foreign Banks"; University of Connecticut Economics Working Paper 2012-02. Chapter V of the book.

72   See Banga and Kumar (2010)